THE EAR OF
THE OTHER

OTOBIOGRAPHIES

The Teaching of Nietzsche and the Politics of the Proper Name

JACQUES DERRIDA
Translated by Avital Ronell

Texts and Discussions
with JACQUES DERRIDA

THE EAR OF
THE OTHER

Otobiography, Transference, Translation

English edition edited by
Christie V. McDonald
(*Based on the French edition edited by Claude*
Lévesque and Christie V. McDonald)

Translated by Peggy Kamuf

SCHOCKEN BOOKS · NEW YORK

To the memory of Eugenio Donato

First published by Schocken Books 1985
10 9 8 7 6 5 4 3 2 1   85 86 87 88
Copyright © 1985 by Schocken Books Inc.
Originally published in French as *L'oreille de l'autre* by V1b Editeur;
   © V1b Editeur, Montreal, 1982

Library of Congress Cataloging in Publication Data
Derrida, Jacques.
   The ear of the other.
   Translation of: L'oreille de l'autre.
   Bibliography: p.
   1.Autobiography—Congresses. 2.Translating
and interpreting—Congresses. I. Lévesque, Claude.
II. McDonald, Christie V. III. Title.
CT25.D4713. 1985   809   84–16053

Designed by Nancy Dale Muldoon
Manufactured in the United States
ISBN 0–8052–3953–7

Contents

Preface

THIS BOOK started on its way to Schocken Books when its president, Julius Glaser, happened onto several pages from the manuscript of an article (dealing with the translation of Jacques Derrida's *Of Grammatology* into English) in a post office on a small island off the coast of Maine where he summers. Sleuthing the origins of the piece, from which the name of the author was mysteriously missing (having been accidentally scattered across an open field, retrieved, and exposed for the author to reclaim), Glaser soon identified the writer and became fascinated with the impact that Derrida's thought was to have on American readers. In the curious entanglement of chance and necessity, it now seems no accident that Schocken Books should publish a book in which Derrida, as one of the leading interpreters of Friedrich Nietzsche, sets the stage for new and important readings of this enigmatic and controversial philosopher, and engages with a number of interlocutors in a form of active interpretation.

This book is the result of a series of meetings held at the University of Montreal from October 22 to 24, 1979. My colleague Claude Lévesque and I invited Jacques Derrida to come to Montreal to meet across the table with several academic professionals in philosophy, psychoanalysis, and literature and to discuss their questions about aspects of philosophy.

From the conversations, which were taped and transcribed, we shaped the book in its present form, making only minor modifications of what had taken place.

The book has three parts, which follow the chronology of the sessions. The first is a lecture by Jacques Derrida entitled "Otobiographies." In it, Derrida deals with two important but rarely juxtaposed texts: Nietzsche's autobiography, *Ecce Homo*, and *On the Future of Our Educational Institutions*. Through them, he discusses the structure of the ear (as a perceiving organ), autobiography, and interpretation: how Nietzsche defers the meaning of his texts so that his signature (as that which validates a check or document—here a book) can come to be understood, honored as it were, only when a reader allies himself with him and, as a receiving ear, signs the text—posthumously. "In other words . . . it is the ear of the other that signs. The ear of the other says me to me. . . . When, much later, the other will have perceived with a keen-enough ear what I will have addressed or destined to him, or her, then my signature will have taken place." And this analysis begins the cautious elaboration of the grounds upon which political readings of Nietzsche's pedagogy might emerge, readings different from those that have made of him predominantly a Nazi. The readings of Nietzsche's texts are not finished, Derrida argues: the same language, the same words, may be read by actively opposed forces. Such a transformative view of reading, as the incessant rewriting of other texts, marks the prolongation of the fundamental strategy of deconstruction (as developed in earlier works: *Of Grammatology*, *Writing and Difference*, *Dissemination*, and *Margins of Philosophy*), in which no text can be reduced to a single meaning.

The second part of the book is a roundtable of several participants discussing notions of what constitutes autobiographical writing: how the *autos* (the self as the subject of biography) has been determined in psychoanalytic, philosophical, and literary terms, and how it might be restructured otherwise. The third part is a similar roundtable on the subject of translation in a wide range of senses, including the formation of languages and meaning (in psychoanalysis, for example), the kinship of languages, philosophy as the translation of a truth in which univocal meaning is possible, et cetera. Everything is questioned; in the complex network of thought concerning autobiography and translation developed here, no original ever remains anywhere intact: neither one's mother tongue, the empirical sense of life, nor what constitutes the feminine.

In addition to 'Otobiographies," two other texts served as specific points of reference for the discussion: "Me—Psychoanalysis: An Introduction to the Translation of 'The Shell and the Kernel' by Nicolas Abraham"; and "Living On: Borderlines." _La Carte postale_ was in press at the time; allusions to it can be found in the discussions of destination and sexual identity.

In the discussions, each participant addresses Jacques Derrida, in most cases about his work, and he then responds. He chose the subjects for discussion, but each of the participants pursues the particular interests of his own work. Eugenio Donato was a professor of comparative literature at the University of California at Irvine; Rodolphe Gasché is a professor of comparative literature at the State University of New York at Buffalo. Several of us teach, or have taught at the University of Montreal: Claude Lévesque is a professor in the Philosophy Department; Patrick Mahony is a professor in the English Department and a practicing psychoanalyst; Christie V. McDonald, a professor in the French Department, is currently Chair of Modern Languages and Classics at Emory University; François Péraldi, a professor in the Linguistics Department, is also a practicing psychoanalyst; and Eugene Vance, formerly a professor in the Program of Comparative Literature, is a professor of Modern Languages at Emory University.

Jacques Derrida was for many years a professor of the history of philosophy at the Ecole Normale Supérieure in Paris; he is now a professor at the Ecole des Hautes Etudes en Sciences Sociales. He has wrought his complex and forceful critique of writing within the Western tradition by rereading the works of writers from Plato to our time. In this vast project, always scrupulously exacting in its analyses, he has "re-marked" the theoretical insufficiency of conceptual thinking and of concepts in the way we ordinarily refer to them: one of these is the concept of context. A written sign, he notes, carries with it a force of breaking with its context, and this "force of breaking is not an accidental predicate, but the very structure of the written." The force of this rupture plays itself out rhetorically in what Nietzsche called a change of style he deemed to be plural. The style of this event is a written dialogue in many voices. Because of the diversity of the interests and backgrounds of the participants, because of the particular linguistic character of the place where the discussions were held (Quebec), and in keeping with the rules of the genre, it seems that our questions were bound to displace the context of Jacques Derrida's responses—as much from the French milieu out of which they grew as from the ongoing American debate toward which they are now directed. That he was brought to formulate certain arguments which can be found as yet nowhere else in published form adds, we believe, to the interest and the richness of this text.

CHRISTIE V. MCDONALD
Cranberry Island, Maine

August 1984

Translator's Note

WITH VERY few exceptions, the English translation of "Otobiographies" by Jacques Derrida, which was done with Avital Ronell, preserves all of the German included in Derrida's text. The passages from *Ecce Homo* and *Thus Spake Zarathustra* are taken, with only slight modification, from Walter Kaufmann's translations. The other Nietzsche text quoted extensively, *On the Future of Our Educational Institutions*, is cited here in a frequently modified version of the extant English translation, first published in 1909, by J. M. Kennedy.

The two roundtable discussions also include frequent reference to other texts and extensive quotation. Whenever possible, such quotations have been drawn from published translations. So as to neither clutter the bottom of the page with references to these translations nor omit such references, a list of works cited has been appended at the end of the volume. All quotations from texts by Derrida which have yet to appear in English translation (e.g., *Glas*) have been translated only for this context.

English readers encountering Derrida's writing for the first time may be disconcerted by the dense mixing of styles, the demanding syntax, and a lexicon that expands the limits of the most unabridged dictionary. Of these lexical supplements, the term *differance*—which occurs several times in the following pages—requires special mention, although the full implications of its use within Derrida's thought cannot be summarized here. (The reader is referred to the essay "Différance" in *Margins of Philosophy* [1982].) Derrida forges this word at the intersection of the spatial and temporal senses of the verb *différer:* to differ and to defer. The standard spelling of the noun *différence* corresponds only to the first, spatial sense; there is no standard noun formed from the second sense of temporal deferral. The *-ance* ending conforms to the orthographics of a middle voice: neither active, nor passive, both active and passive (as in resonance). With the term, Derrida designates the movement of differentiation and deferral, spacing and temporalization which must be thought of as preceding and comprehending any positioning of identifiable differences or oppositions. Significantly for Derrida's deconstruction of the traditional, philosophical opposition of speech and writing, the difference between *différence* and *différance* is unpronounced.

   An occasional translator's note punctuates the following pages whenever it seemed worth the risk of distracting the reader. All other footnotes are the author's or editor's.

PEGGY KAMUF
Miami University

OTOBIOGRAPHIES

The Teaching of Nietzsche and the Politics of the Proper Name

JACQUES DERRIDA
Translated by Avital Ronell

1. Logic of the Living Feminine

". . . for there are human beings who lack everything, except one thing of which they have too much—human beings who are nothing but a big eye or a big mouth or a big belly or anything at all that is big. Inverse cripples [umgekehrte Krüppel] I call them.

"And when I came out of my solitude and crossed over this bridge for the first time I did not trust my eyes and looked and looked again, and said at last, 'An ear! An ear as big as a man!' I looked still more closely—and indeed, underneath the ear something was moving, something pitifully small and wretched and slender. And, no doubt of it, the tremendous ear was attached to a small, thin stalk—but this stalk was a human being! If one used a magnifying glass one could even recognize a tiny envious face; also, that a bloated little soul was dangling from the stalk. The people, however, told me that this great ear was not only a human being, but a great one, a genius. But I never believed the people when they spoke of great men; and I maintained my belief that it was an inverse cripple who had too little of everything and too much of one thing."

When Zarathustra had spoken thus to the hunchback and to those whose mouthpiece and advocate [Mundstück and Fürsprecher] the hunchback was, he turned to his disciples in profound dismay and said: "Verily, my friends, I walk among men as among the fragments and limbs of men [Bruchstücken und Gliedmassen]. This is what is terrible for my eyes, that I find man in ruins [zerstrümmert] and scattered [zerstreut] as over a battlefield or a butcher-field [Schlacht-und Schlächterfeld]. ("On Redemption," Thus Spake Zarathustra)

I would like to spare you the tedium, the waste of time, and the subservience that always accompany the classic pedagogical procedures of forging links, referring back to prior premises or arguments, justifying one's own trajectory, method, system, and more or less skillful transitions, reestablishing continuity, and so on. These are but some of the imperatives of classical pedagogy with which, to be sure, one can never break once and for all. Yet, if you were to submit to them rigorously, they would very soon reduce you to silence, tautology, and tiresome repetition.

I therefore propose *my* compromise to you. And, as everyone knows, by the terms of *academic freedom*—I repeat: a-cademic free-dom—you can take it or leave it. Considering the time I have at my disposal, the tedium I also want to spare myself, the freedom of which I am capable and which I want to preserve, I shall proceed in a manner that some will find aphoristic or inadmissible, that others will accept as law, and that still others will judge to be not quite aphoristic enough. All will be listening to me with one or the other sort of ear (everything comes down to the ear you are able to hear me with) to which the coherence and continuity of my trajectory will have seemed evident from my first words, even from my title. In any case, let us agree to hear and understand one another on this point: whoever no longer wishes to follow may do so. I do not teach truth as such; I do not transform myself into a diaphanous mouthpiece of eternal pedagogy. I settle accounts, however I can, on a certain number of problems: with you and with me or me, and through you, me, and me, with a certain number of authorities represented here. I understand that the place I am now occupying will not be left out of the exhibit or withdrawn from the scene. Nor do I intend to withold even that which I shall call, to save time, an *autobiographical* demonstration, although I must ask you to shift its sense a little and to listen to it with another ear. I wish to take a certain pleasure in this, so that *you may learn this pleasure from me.*

The said "academic freedom," the ear, and autobiography are my objects—for this afternoon.

A discourse on life/death must occupy a certain space between *logos* and *gramme*, analogy and program, as well as between the differing senses of program and reproduction. And since life is on the line, the trait that relates the logical to the graphical must also be working between the biological and biographical, the thanatological and thantographical.

As you know, all these matters are currently undergoing a reevaluation—all these matters, that is to say, the biographical and the *autos* of the autobiographical.

We no longer consider the biography of a "philosopher" as a corpus of empirical accidents that leaves both a name and a signature outside a system which would itself be offered up to an immanent philosophical reading—the only kind of reading held to be philosophically legitimate. This academic notion utterly ignores the demands of a text which it tries to control with the most traditional determinations of what constitutes the limits of the written, or even of "publication." In return for having accepted these limits, one can then and on the other hand proceed to write "lives of philosophers," those biographical novels (complete with style flourishes and character development) to which great historians of philosophy occasionally resign themselves. Such biographical novels or psychobiographies claim that, by following empirical procedures of the psychologistic—at times even psychoanalystic—historicist, or sociologistic type, one can give an account of the genesis of the philosophical system. We say no to this because a new problematic of the biographical in general and of the biography of philosophers in particular must mobilize other resources, including, at the very least, a new analysis of the proper name and the signature. Neither "immanent" readings of philosophical systems (whether such readings be structural or not) nor external, empirical-genetic readings have ever in themselves questioned the *dynamis* of that borderline between the "work" and the "life," the system and the subject of the system. This borderline—I call it *dynamis* because of its force, its power, as well as its virtual and mobile potency—is neither active nor passive, neither outside nor inside. It is most especially not a thin line, an invisible or *indivisible* trait lying between the enclosure of philosophemes, on the one hand, and the life of an author already identifiable behind the name, on the other. This divisible borderline traverses two "bodies," the corpus and the body, in accordance with laws that we are only beginning to catch sight of.

What one calls life—the thing or object of biology and biography—does not stand face to face with something that would be its opposable ob-ject: death, the thanatological or thanatographical. This is the first complication. Also, it is *painfully difficult* for life to become an object of science, in the sense that philosophy and science have always given to the word "science" and to the legal status of scientificity. All of this—the difficulty, the delays it entails—is particularly bound up with the fact that the science of life always accommodates a philosophy of life, which is not the case for all other sciences, the sciences of nonlife—in other words, the sciences of the dead. This might lead one to say that all sciences that win their claim to scientificity without delay or residue are sciences of the dead; and, further, that there is, between the dead and the status of the scientific object, a co-implication which *interests* us, and which concerns the desire to know. If such is the case, then the so-called living subject of biological discourse is a part—an interested party or a partial interest—of the whole field of investment that includes the enormous philosophical, ideological, and political tradition, with all the forces that are at work in that tradition as well as everything that has its potential in the subjectivity of a biologist or a community of biologists. All these evaluations leave their mark on the scholarly signature and inscribe the bio-graphical within the bio-logical.

The name of Nietzsche is perhaps today, for us in the West, the name of someone who (with the possible exceptions of Freud and, in a different way, Kierkegaard) was alone in treating both philosophy and life, the science and the philosophy of life *with his name and in his name.* He has perhaps been alone in putting his name—his *names*—and his biographies on the line, running thus most of the risks this entails: for "him," for "them," for his lives, his names and their future, and particularly for the political future of what he left to be signed.

How can one avoid taking all this into account when reading these texts? One reads only by taking it into account.

To put one's name on the line (with everything a name involves and which cannot be summed up in a _self_), to stage signatures, to make an immense bio-graphical paraph out of all that one has written on life or death—this is perhaps what he has done and what we have to put on active record. Not so as to guarantee him a return, a profit. In the first place, _he_ is dead—a trivial piece of evidence, but incredible enough when you get right down to it and when the name's genius or genie is still there to make us forget the fact of his death. At the very least, to be dead means that no profit or deficit, no good or evil, whether calculated or not, can _ever return again_ to the bearer of the name. Only the name can inherit, and this is why the name, to be distinguished from the bearer, is always and a priori a dead man's name, a name of death. What returns to the name never returns to the living. Nothing ever comes back to the living. Moreover, we shall not assign him the profit because what he has willed in his name resembles— as do all legacies or, in French, _legs_ (understand this word with whichever ear, in whatever tongue you will)—poisoned milk which has, as we shall see in a moment, gotten mixed up in advance with the worst of our times. And it did not get mixed up in this by accident.

Before turning to any of his writings, let it be said that I shall not read Nietzsche as a philosopher (of being, of life, or of death) or as a scholar or scientist, if these three types can be said to share the abstraction of the bio-graphical and the claim to leave their lives and names out of their writings. For the moment, I shall read Nietzsche beginning with the scene from _Ecce Homo_ where he puts his body and his name out front even though he advances behind masks or pseudonyms without proper names. He advances behind a plurality of masks or names that, like any mask and even any theory of the simulacrum, can propose and produce themselves only by returning a constant yield of protection, a surplus value in which one may still recognize the ruse of life. However, the ruse starts incurring losses as soon as the surplus value does not return again to the living, but to and in the name of names, the community of masks.

The point of departure for my reading will be what says "*Ecce Homo*" or what says "*Ecce Homo*" of itself, as well as "*Wie man wird, was man ist*," how one becomes what one is. I shall start with the preface to *Ecce Homo* which is, you could say, coextensive with Nietzsche's entire oeuvre, so much so that the entire oeuvre also prefaces *Ecce Home* and finds itself repeated in the few pages of what one calls, in the strict sense, the Preface to the work entitled *Ecce Homo*. You may know these first lines by heart:

Seeing that before long I must confront humanity with the most diffi-cult demand that has ever been made of it, it seems indispensable to me to say, who I am [*wer ich bin* is italicized]. Really, one should know it, for I have not left myself "without testimony." But the disproportion between the greatness of my task and the *smallness* of my contemporaries has found expression in the fact that one has neither heard nor even seen me. I live on my own credit [I go along living on my own credit, the credit I establish and give myself; *Ich lebe auf meinen eigenen Kredit hin*]; it is perhaps a mere prejudice that I live [*vielleicht bloss ein Vorurteil dass ich lebe*].

His own identity—the one he means to declare and which, being so out of proportion with his contemporaries, has noth-ing to do with what they know by this name, behind his name or rather his homonym, Friedrich Nietzsche—the identity he lays claim to here is not his by right of some contract drawn up with his contemporaries. It has passed to him through the unheard-of contract he has drawn up with himself. He has taken out a loan with himself and *has implicated us in this transaction through what, on the force of a signature, remains of his text. "Auf meinen eigenen Kredit."* It is also our busi-ness, this unlimited credit that cannot be measured against the credit his contemporaries extended or refused him under the name of F.N. Already a false name, a pseudonym and homo-nym, F.N. dissimulates, perhaps, behind the imposter, the other Friedrich Nietzsche. Tied up with this shady business of contracts, debt, and credit, the pseudonym induces us to be

immeasurably wary whenever we think we are reading Nietzsche's signature or "autograph," and whenever he *declares:*
I, the undersigned, F.N.

He never knows in the present, with present knowledge or
even in the present of *Ecce Homo,* whether anyone will ever
honor the inordinate credit that he extends to *himself* in his
name, but also necessarily in the name of another. The consequences of this are not difficult to foresee: if the life that he
lives and tells to himself ("autobiography," they call it) cannot
be *his* life in the first place except as the effect of a secret
contract, a credit account which has been both opened and
encrypted, an indebtedness, an alliance or annulus, then as
long as the contract has not been honored—and it cannot be
honored except by another, for example, by you—Nietzsche
can write that his life is perhaps a mere prejudice, "*es ist
vielleicht bloss ein Vorurteil dass ich lebe.*" A prejudice: life.
Or perhaps not so much life in general, but *my* life, this "that I
live," the "I-live" in the present. It is a prejudgment, a sentence, a hasty arrest, a risky prediction. This life will be verified only at the moment the bearer of the name, the one whom
we, in our prejudice, call living, will have died. It will be
verified only at some moment after or during death's arrest.*
And if life returns, it will return to the name but not to the
living, in the name of the living *as* a name of the dead.

"He" has proof of the fact that the "I live" is a prejudgment
(and thus, due to the effect of murder which a priori follows, a
harmful prejudice) linked to the bearing of the name and to
the structure of all proper names. He says that he has proof
every time he questions one of the ranking "educated" men
who come to the Upper Engadine. As Nietzsche's name is
unknown to any of them, he who calls himself "Nietzsche"
then holds proof of the fact that he does not live presently: "I
live on my own credit; it is perhaps a mere prejudice that I
live. I need only speak with one of the 'educated' who come to
the Upper Engadine . . . and I am convinced that I do *not* live

---

**Arrêt de mort:* both death sentence and reprieve from death.—Tr.

[*das ich lebe nicht*]. Under these circumstances I have a duty against which my habits, even more the pride of my instincts, revolt at bottom—namely, to say: *Hear me! For I am such and such a person* [literally: I am he and he, *ich bin der und der*]. *Above all, do not mistake me for someone else."* All of this is emphasized.

He says this unwillingly, but he has a "duty" to say so in order to acquit himself of a debt. To whom?

Forcing himself to say who he is, he goes against his natural *habitus* that prompts him to dissimulate behind masks. You know, of course, that Nietzsche constantly affirms the value of dissimulation. Life is dissimulation. In saying "*ich bin der und der*," he seems to be going against the instinct of dissimulation. This might lead us to believe that, *on the one hand*, his contract goes against his nature: it is by doing violence to himself that he promises to honor a pledge in the name of the name, in his name and in the name of the other. *On the other hand*, however, this auto-presentative exhibition of the "*ich bin der und der*" could well be still a ruse of dissimulation. We would again be mistaken if we understood it as a simple presentation of identity, assuming that we already know what is involved in self-presentation and a statement of identity ("Me, such a person," male or female, an individual or collective subject, "Me, psychoanalysis," "Me, metaphysics").

Everything that will subsequently be said about truth will have to be reevaluated on the basis of this question and this anxiety. As if it were not already enough to unsettle our theoretical certainties about identity and what we think we know about a proper name, very rapidly, on the following page, Nietzsche appeals to his "experience" and his "wanderings in forbidden realms." They have taught him to consider the causes of idealization and moralization in an entirely different light. He has seen the dawning of a "*hidden* history" of philosophers—*he does not say of philosophy*—and the "psychology of their great names."

Let us assume, in the first place, that the "I live" is guaranteed by a nominal contract which falls due only upon the death of the one who says "I live" in the present; further, let us assume that the relationship of a philosopher to his "great name"—that is, to what borders a system of his signature—is a matter of psychology, but a psychology so novel that it would no longer be legible _within_ the system of philosophy as one of its parts, nor within psychology considered as a region of the philosophical encyclopedia. Assuming, then, that all this is stated in the Preface signed "Friedrich Nietzsche" to a book entitled _Ecce Homo_—a book whose final words are "Have I been understood? _Dionysus versus the Crucified"_ [ge- gen den Gekreuzigten], Nietzsche, Ecce Homo, Christ but not Christ, nor even Dionysus, but rather the name of the _versus_, the adverse or countername, the combat called between the two names—this would suffice, would it not, to pluralize in a singular fashion the proper name and the homonymic mask? It would suffice, that is, to lead all the affiliated threads of the name astray in a labyrinth which is, of course, the labyrinth of the ear. Proceed, then, by seeking out the edges, the inner walls, the passages.

Between the Preface signed F.N., which comes after the title, and the first chapter, "Why I Am So Wise," there is a single page. It is an outwork, an _hors d'oeuvre,_ an exergue or a flysheet whose _topos,_ like (its) temporality, strangely dislo- cates the very thing that we, with our untroubled assurance, would like to think of as the time of life and the time of life's récit,* of the writing of life by the living—in short, the time of autobiography.

The page is dated. To date is to sign. And to "date from" is also to indicate the place of the signature. This page is in a certain way dated because it says "today" and today "my birthday," the anniversary of my birth. The anniversary is the moment when the year turns back on itself, forms a ring or annulus with itself, annuls itself and begins anew. It is here: my forty-fifth year, the day of the year when I am forty-five

---

*Rather than attempt to translate this word as "account" or "story" or "narration," it has been left in French throughout.—Tr.

years old, something like the midday of life. The noon of life, even midlife crisis,[†] is commonly situated at about this age, at the shadowless midpoint of a great day.

Here is how the exergue begins: "*An diesem vollkommhen Tage, wo Alles reift*," "On this perfect day when everything is ripening, and not only the grape turns brown, the eye of the sun just fell upon my life [has fallen due as if by chance: *fiel mir eben ein Sonnenblick auf meinen Leben*]."

It is a shadowless moment consonant with all the "middays" of Zarathustra. It comes as a moment of affirmation, returning like the anniversary from which one can look forward and backward at one and the same time. The shadow of all negativity has disappeared: "I looked back, I looked forward, and never saw so many and such good things at once."

Yet, this midday tolls the hour of a burial. Playing on everyday language, he buries his past forty-four years. But what he actually buries is death, and in burying death he has saved life—and immortality. "It was not for nothing that I buried [*begrub*] my forty-fourth year today; I had the *right* to bury it; whatever was life in it has been saved, is immortal. The first book of the *Revaluation of All Values*, the *Songs of Zarathustra*, the *Twilight of the Idols*, my attempt to philosophize with a hammer—all presents [*Geschenke*] of this year, indeed of its last quarter. *How could I fail to be grateful to my whole life?*— and so I tell my life to myself" ["*Und so erzähle ich mir mein Leben*"].

He indeed says: I tell my life *to myself*; I recite and recount it thus *for me*. We have come to the end of the exergue on the flysheet between the Preface and the beginning of *Ecce Homo*.

To receive one's life as a gift, or rather, to be grateful to life for what she gives, for giving after all what is *my* life; more precisely, to recognize one's gratitude to life for such a gift— the gift being what has managed to get written and signed with this name for which I have established my own credit and which will be what it has become only on the basis of

---

[†]"Le démon de midi"; literally, the midday demon.—Tr.

what this year has given me (the three works mentioned in the passage), in the course of the event dated by an annual course of the sun, and even by a part of its course or recourse, its returning—to reaffirm what has occurred during these forty-four years as having been good and as bound to return eternally, immortally: this is what *constitutes,* gathers, adjoins, and holds the strange present of this auto-biographical *récit* in place. "*Und so erzähle ich mir mein Leben.*" This *récit* that buries the dead and saves the saved or exceptional as immortal is not *auto*-biographical for the reason one commonly understands, that is, because the signatory tells the story of his life or the return of his past life as life and not death. Rather, it is because he tells *himself* this life and he is the narration's first, if not its only, addressee and destination—within the text. And since the "I" of this *récit* only constitutes itself though the credit of the eternal return, he does not exist. He does not sign prior to the *récit qua* eternal return. Until then, *until now,* that I am living may be a mere prejudice. It is the eternal return that signs or seals.

Thus, you cannot think the name or names of Friedrich Nietzsche, you cannot *hear* them before the reaffirmation of the hymen, before the alliance or wedding ring of the eternal return. You will not understand anything of his life, nor of his life and works, until you hear the thought of the "yes, yes" given to this shadowless gift at the ripening high noon, beneath that division whose borders are inundated by sunlight: the overflowing cup of the sun. Listen again to the overture of *Zarathustra.*

This is why it is so difficult to determine the *date* of such an event. How can one situate the advent of an auto-biographical *récit* which, as the thought of the eternal return, requires that we let the advent of all events come about in another way? This difficulty crops up wherever one seeks to make a *determination:* in order to date an event, of course, but also in order to identify the beginning of a text, the origin of life, or the first movement of a signature. These are all problems of the borderline.

Without fail, the structure of the exergue on the borderline or of the borderline in the exergue will be reprinted wherever the question of life, of "my-life," arises. Between a title or a preface on the one hand, and the book to come on the other, between the title *Ecce Homo* and *Ecce Homo* "itself," the structure of the exergue situates the place from which life will be *recited*, that is to say, reaffirmed—*yes, yes, amen, amen*. It is life that has to return eternally (selectively, as the living feminine and not as the dead that resides within her and must be buried), as life allied to herself by the nuptial annulus, the wedding ring. This *place* is to be found neither in the work (it is an exergue) nor in the life of the author. At least it is not there in a simple fashion, but neither is it simply exterior to them. It is in this place that affirmation is repeated: yes, yes, I approve, I sign, I subscribe to this acknowledgment of the debt incurred toward "myself," "my-life"—and I want it to return. Here, at noon, the least shadow of all negativity is buried. The design of the exergue reappears later, in the chapter "Why I Write Such Good Books," where Nietzsche's preparations for the "great noon" are made into a commitment, a debt, a "duty," "my duty of preparing a moment of the highest self-examination for human-ity, a *great noon* when it looks back and far forward [*wo sie zurückschaut und hinausschaut*]" ("Dawn").

But the noon of life is not a place and it does not take place. For that very reason, it is not a moment but only an instantly vanishing limit. What is more, it returns every day, always, each day, with every turn of the annulus. Always before noon, after noon. If one has the right to read F.N.'s signature only at this instant—the instant in which he signs "noon, yes, yes, I and I who recite my life to myself"—well, you can see what an impossible protocol this implies for reading and especially for teaching, as well as what ridiculous naiveté, what sly, obscure, and shady business are behind declarations of the type: Fried-rich Nietzsche said this or that, he thought this or that about this or that subject—about life, for example, in the sense of human or biological existence—Friedrich Nietzsche or who-ever after noon, such-and-such a person. Me, for example.

I shall not read *Ecce Homo* with you. I leave you with this forewarning or foreword about the place of the exergue and the fold that it forms along the lines of an inconspicuous limit: There is no more shadow, and all statements, before and after, left and right, are at once possible (Nietzsche said it all, more or less) and necessarily contradictory (he said the most mutually incompatible things, and he said that he said them). Yet, before leaving *Ecce Homo*, let us pick up just one hint of this contradicting duplicity.

What happens right after this sort of exergue, after this date? (It is, after all, a *date:** signature, anniversary reminder, celebration of gifts or givens, acknowledgment of debt.) After this "date," the first chapter ("Why I Am So Wise") begins, as you know, with the origins of "my" life: my father and my mother. In other words, once again, the principle of contradiction in my life which falls between the principles of death and life, the end and the beginning, the high and the low, degeneracy and ascendancy, et cetera. This contradiction is my fatality. And my fatality derives from my very genealogy, from my father and mother, from the fact that I decline, in the form of a riddle, as my parents' identity. In a word, my dead father, my living mother, my father the dead man or death, my mother the living feminine or life. As for me, I am between the two: this lot has fallen to me, it is a "chance," a throw of the dice; and at this place my truth, my double truth, takes after both of them. These lines are well known:

> The good fortune of my existence [*Das Glück meines Daseins*], its uniqueness perhaps [he says "perhaps," and thereby he reserves the possibility that this chancy situation may have an exemplary or paradigmatic character], lies in its fatality: I am, to express it in the form of a riddle [*Rätselform*], already dead as my father [*als mein Vater bereits gestorben*], while as my mother, I am still living and becoming old [*als meine Mutter lebe ich noch und werde alt*].

---

*From "*data littera*," "letter given," the first words of a medieval formula indicating the time and place of a legal act.—Tr.

Inasmuch as *I am and follow after* my father, I am the dead man and I am death. Inasmuch as *I am and follow after* my mother, I am life that perseveres, I am the living and the living feminine. I am my father, my mother, and me, and me who is my father my mother and me, my son and me, death and life, the dead man and the living feminine, and so on.

There, this is who I am, a certain masculine and a certain feminine. *Ich bin der und der*, a phrase which means all these things. You will not be able to hear and understand my name unless you hear it with an ear attuned to the name of the dead man and the living feminine—the double and divided name of the father who is dead and the mother who is living on, who will moreover outlive me long enough to bury me. The mother is living on, and this living on is the name of the mother. This survival is my life whose shores she overflows. And my father's name, in other words, my patronym? That is the name of my death, of my dead life.

Must one not take this unrepresentable scene into account each time one claims to identify any utterance signed by F.N.? The utterances I have just read or translated do not belong to the genre of autobiography in the strict sense of the term. To be sure, it is not wrong to say that Nietzsche speaks of his "real" (as one says) father and mother. But he speaks of them "*in Rätselform*," symbolically, by way of a riddle; in other words, in the form of a proverbial legend, and as a story that has a lot to teach.

What, then, are the consequences of this double origin? The birth of Nietzsche, in the double sense of the word "birth" (the act of being born and family lineage), is itself double. It brings something into the world and the light of day out of a singular couple: death and life, the dead man and the living feminine, the father and the mother. The double birth explains who I am and how I determine my identity: as double and neutral.

This double descent [*Diese doppelte Herkunft*], as it were, from both the highest and the lowest rungs on the ladder of life, at the same time *décadent* and a *beginning*—this, if anything, explains that neutrality, that freedom from all partiality in relation to the total problem of life, that perhaps distinguishes me. I have a subtler sense of smell [pay attention to what he repeatedly says about hunting, trails, and his nostrils] for the signs of ascent and decline [literally of rising and setting, as one says of the sun: *für die Zeichen von Aufgang und Niedergang*; of that which climbs and declines, of the high and the low] than any other human being before. I am the master *par excellence* for this—I know both, I am both [*ich kenne beides, ich bin beides*].

I am a master, I am the master, the teacher [*Lehrer*] "*par excellence*" (the latter words in French, as is *décadent* earlier in the passage). I know and I am the both of them (one would have to read "the both" as being in the singular), the dual or the double, I know what I am, the both, the two, life the dead [*la vie le mort*]. Two, and from them one gets life the dead. When I say "Do not mistake me for someone else, I am *der und der*," this is what I mean: the dead the living, the dead man the living feminine.

The alliance that Nietzsche follows in turning his signature into riddles links the logic of the dead to that of the living feminine. It is an alliance in which he seals or forges his signatures—and he also simulates them: the demonic neutrality of midday delivered from the negative and from dialectic.

"I know both, I am both.—My father died at the age of thirty-six. He was delicate, kind and morbid, as a being that is destined merely to pass by [*wie ein nur zum Vorübergehn bestimmtes Wesen*]—more a gracious memory of life rather than life itself." It is not only that the son does not survive his father *after* the latter's death, but the father was *already* dead; he will have died during his own life. As a "living" father, he was already only the memory of life, of an already prior life. Elsewhere, I have related this elementary kinship structure (of a dead or rather absent father, already absent to himself, and of the mother living above and after all, living on long enough to bury the one she has brought into the world, an ageless virgin inaccessible to all ages) to a logic of the death knell [*glas*] and of *obsequence*. There are examples of this logic in some of the best families, for example, the family of Christ (with whom Dionysus stands face to face, but as his specular double). There is also Nietzsche's family, if one considers that the mother survived the "breakdown." In sum and in general, if one "sets aside all the facts," the logic can be found in all families.

Before the cure or resurrection which he also recounts in *Ecce Homo*, this only son will have first of all repeated his father's death: "In the same year in which his life went downward, mine, too, went downward: at thirty-six I reached the lowest point of my vitality—I still lived, but without being able to see three steps ahead. Then—it was 1879—I retired from my professorship at Basel, spent the summer in St. Moritz like a shadow and the next winter, the most sunless of my life, in Naumberg as a shadow. This was my minimum. The *Wanderer and His Shadow* was born at this time. Doubtless I then knew about shadows." A little further, we read: "My readers know perhaps in what way I consider dialectic as a symptom of decadence; for example in the most famous case, the case of Socrates." *Im Fall des Sokrates*: one might also say in his *casus*, his expiration date and his decadence. He is a Socrates, that *décadent par excellence*, but he is also the reverse. This is what he makes clear at the beginning of the next section: "Taking into account that I am a *décadent*, I am also the opposite." The double provenance, already mentioned at the beginning of section 1, then reaffirmed and explained in section 2, may also be heard at the opening of section 3: "This *dual* series of experiences, this access to apparently separate worlds, is repeated in my nature in every respect: I am a *Doppelgänger*, I have a 'second' sight in addition to the first. *And* perhaps also a third." Second and third sight. Not only, as he says elsewhere, a third ear. Only a moment ago, he has explained to us that in tracing the portrait of the "well-turned-out person" [*wohlgerathner Mensch*] he has just described himself: "Well, then, I am the *opposite* of a *décadent*, for I have just described myself."

The contradiction of the "double" thus goes beyond whatever declining negativity might accompany a dialectical opposition. What counts in the final accounting and beyond what can be counted is a certain *step beyond*.* I am thinking here of Maurice Blanchot's syntaxless syntax in his *Pas au-delà* ["The Step Beyond"]. There, he approaches death in what I would call a step-by-step procedure of overstepping or of impossible transgression. *Ecce Homo:* "In order to understand anything at all of my *Zarathustra*, one must perhaps be similarly conditioned as I am—with one foot *beyond* life." A foot,[†] and going beyond the opposition between life and/or death, a single step.

2. The Otograph Sign of State

The autobiography's signature is written in this step. It remains a line of credit opened onto eternity and refers back to one of the two I's, the nameless parties to the contract, only according to the annulus of the eternal return.

This does not prevent—on the contrary, it allows—the person who says "I am noon in the fullness of summer" ("Why I Am So Wise") also to say "I am double. Therefore, I do not mistake myself, at least not yet for my works."

There is here a differance of autobiography, an allo- and thanatography. Within this differance, it is precisely the question of the institution—the teaching institution—that gives a new account of itself. It is to this question, to this institution that I wished to make an introduction.

The good news of the eternal return is a message and a teaching, the address or the destination of a doctrine. By definition, it cannot let itself be heard or understood in the present; it is untimely, differant, and anachronistic. Yet, since this

---

*"*Pas au-delà*," both "step(s) beyond" and "not beyond."—Tr.

†The death of the father, blindness, the foot: one may be wondering why I am not speaking here of oedipus or Oedipus. This was intentionally held in reserve for another reading directly concerned with the Nietzschean *thematic* of oedipus and the name of Oedipus.

news repeats an affirmation (yes, yes), since it affirms the return, the rebeginning, and a certain kind of reproduction that preserves whatever comes back, then its very logic must give rise to a magisterial institution. Zarathustra is a master [Lehrer], and as such he dispenses a doctrine and intends to found new institutions.

Institutions of the "yes," which have need of ears. But how so? He says, "*Das eine bin ich, das andre sind meine Schriften.*"

I am one thing, my writings are another matter. Before I discuss them one by one, let me touch upon the question of their being understood or *not* understood. I'll do it as casually as decency permits; for the time for this question certainly hasn't come yet. The time for me hasn't come yet: some of my writings will be born only posthumously.* Some day institutions [*Institutionen*] will be needed in which men live and teach as I conceive of living and teaching; it might even happen that a few chairs will then be set aside [*eigene:* appropriated to] for the interpretation of *Zarathustra.* But it would contradict my character entirely if I expected ears *and hands* for *my* truths today: that today one doesn't hear me and doesn't accept my ideas is not only comprehensible, it even seems right to me. I don't want to be confounded with others—this requires that I do not confuse myself.

The ear, then, is also at stake in teaching and in its new institutions. As you know, everything gets wound up in Nietzsche's ear, in the motifs of his labyrinth. Without getting in any deeper here, I simply note the frequent reappearance of this motif in the same chapter ["Why I Write Such Good Books"] of *Ecce Homo,*† and I right away step back, through

Einige werden posthum geboren; Kaufmann translates this phrase as "Some are born posthumously."—Tr.

†One example among many: "All of us know, even know from experience, what a long-eared beast the ass is [*was ein Langohr ist*]. Well then, I dare assert that I have the smallest ears. This is of no small interest to the little ladies [*Weiblein*]—it seems to me that they may feel I understand them better. I am the *anti-ass par excellence* and thus a world-historical monster—I am, in Greek and not only in Greek, the *Anti-Christ.*"

another effect of the labyrinth, toward a text altogether at the other end, entitled *On the Future of Our Educational Institutions* (1872).

I have, I am, and I demand a keen ear, I am (the) both, (the) double, I sign double, my writings and I make two, I am the (masculine) dead the living (feminine) and I am destined to them, I come from the two of them, I address myself to them, and so on. How does the knot of all these considerations tie up with the tangled politics and policies in *The Future* . . .?

Today's teaching establishment perpetrates a crime against life understood as the living feminine: disfiguration disfigures the maternal tongue, profanation profanes its body.

By nature, everyone nowadays writes and speaks the German tongue as poorly and vulgarly as is possible in the era of journalistic German: that is why the nobly gifted youth should be taken by force and placed under a bell-jar [*Glasglocke*] of good taste and severe linguistic discipline. If this proves impossible, I would prefer a return to spoken Latin because I am ashamed of a language so disfigured and so profaned. . . . Instead of that purely practical method of instruction by which the teacher must accustom his pupils to severe self-discipline in the language, we find everywhere the rudiments of a historico-scholastic method of teaching the mother-tongue: that is to say, people treat it as if it were a dead language and as if one had no obligation to the present or the future of this language. ("Second Lecture")

There is thus a law that creates obligations with regard to language, and particularly with regard to the language in which the law is stated: the mother tongue. This is the living language (as opposed to Latin, a dead, paternal language, the language of another law where a secondary repression has set in—the law of death). There has to be a pact or alliance with the living language and language of the living feminine against death, against the dead. The repeated affirmation—like the contract, hymen, and alliance—always belongs to language: it comes down and comes back to the signature of the maternal, nondegenerate, noble tongue. The detour through *Ecce Homo*

will have given us this to think about: History or historical
science, which puts to death or treats the dead, which deals or
negotiates with the dead, is the science of the father. It occu-
pies the place of the dead and the place of the father. To be
sure, the master, even the good master, is also a father, as is
the master who prefers Latin to bad German or to the mis-
treated mother. Yet the good master trains for the service of
the mother whose subject he is; he commands obedience by
obeying the law of the mother tongue and by respecting the
living integrity of its body.

The historical method has become so universal in our time, that even
the living body of language [*der lebendige Leib der Sprache*] is sacrificed to its anatomical study. But this is precisely where culture
[*Bildung*] begins—namely, in understanding how to treat the living
as living [*das Lebendige als lebendig*], and it is here too that the
mission of the master of culture begins: in suppressing 'historical
interest' which tries to impose itself there where one must above all
else act [*handeln*: to treat or handle] correctly rather than know correctly [*richtig*]. Our mother-tongue is a domain in which the pupil
must learn to act correctly.

The law of the mother, as language, is a "domain" [*Gebiet*],
a living body not to be "sacrificed" or given up [*preisgeben*]
dirt-cheap. The expression "*sich preisgeben*" can also mean to
give or abandon oneself for a nominal fee, even to prostitute
oneself. The master must suppress the movement of this mis-
treatment inflicted on the body of the mother tongue, this
letting go at any price. He must learn to treat the living feminine correctly.

These considerations will guide my approach to this "youthful work" (as they say) on the *Future of Our Educational Institutions*. In this place of a very dense crisscrossing of questions,
we must approach selectively, moving between the issue of the
pedagogical institution, on the one hand, and, on the other,
those concerning life–death, the-dead-the-living, the language
contract, the signature of credit, the biological, and the biographical. The detour taken through *Ecce Homo* will serve, in

both a paradoxical and a prudent manner, as our protocol. I shall not invoke the notion of an "already," nor will I attempt to illuminate the "youthful" with a teleological insight in the form of a "lesson." Yet, without giving such a retro-perspective the sense that it has acquired in the Aristotelian-Hegelian tradition, we may be able to fall back on what Nietzsche himself teaches about the line of "credit" extended to a signature, about delaying the date of expiration, about the posthumous difference between him and his work, et cetera. This of course complicates the protocols of reading with respect to The Future. . . .

I give notice at the onset that I shall not mulitply these protocols in order to dissimulate whatever embarrassment might arise from this text. That is, I do not aim to "clear" its "author" and neutralize or defuse either what might be troublesome in it for democratic pedagogy or "leftist" politics, or what served as "language" for the most sinister rallying cries of National Socialism. On the contrary, the greatest indecency is de rigueur in this place. One may even wonder why it is not enough to say: "Nietzsche did not think that," "he did not want that," or "he would have surely vomited this,"* that

---

*I say "vomit" deliberately. Nietzsche constantly draws our attention to the value of learning to vomit, forming in this way one's taste, distaste, and disgust, knowing how to use one's mouth and palate, moving one's tongue and lips, having good teeth or being hard-toothed, understanding how to speak and to eat (but not just anything!). All of this we know, as well as the fact that the word "Ekel" (disgust, nausea, wanting to vomit) comes back again and again to set the stage for evaluation. These are so many questions of styles. It should now be possible for an analysis of the word "Ekel," as well as of everything that it carries down with it, to make way for a hand-to-hand combat between Nietzsche and Hegel within that space so admirably marked out by Werner Hamacher [Pleroma, 1978] between Ekel and Hegel in Hegel's Der Geist des Christentums. In the lectures On the Future of Our Educational Institutions, it is disgust that controls everything—and first of all, in democracy, journalism, the State and its University. For example, following only the lexical occurrences of Ekel: "Only by means of such discipline can the young man acquire that physical loathing [Ekel] for the elegance of style which is so appreciated and valued by those who work in journalism factories and who scribble novels; by it alone is he irrevocably elevated at a stroke above a whole host of absurd questions and scruples, such, for instance, as whether

there is falsification of the legacy and an interpretive mystification going on here. One may wonder how and why what is so naively called a falsification was possible (one can't falsify just anything), how and why the "same" words and the "same" statements—if they are indeed the same—might several times be made to serve certain meanings and certain contexts that are said to be different, even incompatible. One may wonder why the only teaching institution or the only beginning of a teaching institution that ever succeeded in taking as its model the teaching of Nietzsche on teaching will have been a Nazi one.

First protocol: These lectures do not belong simply to the "posthumous" state mentioned by *Ecce Homo*. Had they title to the posthumous, they might have been binding on their author. However, Nietzsche expressly said that he would not want to see the text they constitute published, even after his death. What is more, he interrupted the course of this discourse along the way. I am not saying that he repudiated it entirely or that he repudiated those passages, for instance, that would be most scandalous to any contemporary anti-Nazi democrat. Nevertheless, let's remember that he "swore" not to

[Berthold] Auerbach and [Karl] Gutzkow are really poets, for his disgust [*Ekel*] at both will be so great that he will be unable to read them any longer, and thus the problem will be solved for him. Let no one imagine that it is an easy matter to develop this feeling to the extent necessary in order to have this physical loathing; but let no one hope to reach sound aesthetic judgments along any other road than the thorny one of language, and by this I do not mean philological research, but self-discipline in one's mother-tongue" ("Second Lecture").

Without wishing to exploit the German word "*Signatur*," one could say that Nietzsche's historical disgust is aroused first of all by the signature of his era— that by which his era distinguishes, signifies, characterizes, and identifies itself: namely, the democratic signature. To this signature, Nietzsche opposes another one that is untimely, yet to come and still anachronistic. One could reread the "First Lecture" from this point of view, with particular attention to this passage: "But this belongs to the signature without value [*nichtswürdigen Signatur*] of our present culture. The rights of genius have been democratized so that people may be relieved of the labor by which one forms oneself, and of the personal necessity of culture [*Bildungsarbeit, Bildungsnot*]."

publish these lectures. On July 25, 1872, after the Fifth Lecture, he writes to Wagner that "in the beginning of the coming
winter, I intend to give my Basel audience the sixth and sev-
enth lectures 'on the future of our educational institutions.' I
want at least to *have done with it,* even in the diminished and
inferior form with which I have treated this theme up until
now. To treat it in a *superior* form, I would have to become
more 'mature' and try to educate myself." However, he will
not deliver these two last lectures and will refuse to publish
them. On December 20, he writes to Malvida von Meysenbug:
"By now you will have read these lectures and have been
startled by the story's abrupt ending after such a long prelude
[he is referring to the narrative fiction, the imaginary conver-
sation that opens the first lecture], and to see how the thirst
for genuinely new thoughts and propositions ended up losing
itself in pure negativity and numerous digressions. This reading makes one thirsty and, in the end, there is nothing to
drink! Truthfully, what I set out to do in the final lecture—a
series of nocturnal illuminations filled with extravagances and
colors—was not suitable for my Basel audience, and it was a
good thing the words *never left my mouth*" [italics added].
And toward the end of the following February, he writes:
"You must believe me . . . in a few years I will be able to do
better, and I will want to. In the meantime, these lectures have
for me the value of an exhortation: they call me to a duty and
a task that are distinctly incumbent upon me. . . . These lectures are summary and, what is more, a bit improvised. . . .
Fritsch was prepared to publish them, but I swore not to publish any book that doesn't leave me with a conscience as clear
as an angel's."

Other protocol: One must allow for the "genre" whose code
is constantly re-marked, for narrative and fictional form and
the "indirect style." In short, one must allow for all the ways
intent ironizes or demarcates itself, demarcating the text by
leaving on it the mark of genre. These lectures, given by an
academic to academics and students on the subject of studies
in the university and secondary school, amount to a theatrical

infraction of the laws of genre and academicism. For lack of time, I will not analyze these traits in themselves. However, we should not ignore the invitation extended to us in the Preface to the lectures where we are asked to read slowly, like anachronistic readers who escape the law of their time by taking time to read—all the time it takes, without saying "for lack of time" as I have just done. These are the terms that will enable one to read between the lines, as he asks us to do, but also to read without trying to preserve "ancient rules" as one usually does. This requires a *meditatio generis futuri*, a practical meditation which goes so far as to give itself time for an effective destruction of the secondary school and university. "What must happen between the time when new legislators, in the service of a totally new culture, will be born and the present time? Perhaps the destruction of the *Gymnasium* [the German secondary school], perhaps even the destruction of the university or, at the very least, a transformation of these teaching establishments which will be so total that their ancient rules will seem in the eyes of the future to be the remains of a cave-dwellers' civilization." In the meantime, Nietzsche advises us, as he will do in the case of *Zarathustra*, to forget and destroy the text, but to forget and destroy it through action.

Taking into account the present scene, how shall I in turn sift through this text? And what is to be retained of it?

In the first place, a phoenix motif. Once again, the destruction of life is only an appearance; it is the destruction of the appearance of life. One buries or burns what is *already dead* so that life, the living feminine, will be reborn and regenerated from these ashes. The vitalist theme of degeneration/regeneration is active and central throughout the argument. This revitalization, as we have already seen, must first of all pass by way of the tongue, that is, by way of the exercise of the tongue or language, the *treatment* of its body, the mouth and the ear, passing between the natural, living mother tongue and the scientific, formal, dead paternal language. And since it is a question of treatment, this necessarily involves education, training, discipline. The annihilation [*Vernichtung*] of the gymnasium has to prepare the grounds for a renaissance [*Neugeburt*]. (The most recurrent theme in the lectures is that the university, regardless of its opinion in the matter, is nothing but the product or further development of what has been preformed or programmed at the secondary school.) The act of destruction destroys only that which, being already degenerated, offers itself selectively to annihilation. The expression "degeneration" designates both the loss of vital, genetic, or generous forces and the loss of *kind*, either species or genre: the *Entartung*. Its frequent recurrence characterizes culture, notably university culture once it has become state-controlled and journalistic. This concept of degeneration has—*already*, you could say—the structure that it "will" have in later analyses, for example in *The Genealogy of Morals*. Degeneration does not let life dwindle away through a regular and continual decline and according to some homogeneous process. Rather, it is touched off by an inversion of values when a hostile and reactive principle actually becomes the active enemy of life. The degenerate is not a lesser vitality; it is a life principle hostile to life.

The word "degeneration" proliferates particularly in the fifth and last lecture, where the conditions for the regenerative leap are defined. Democratic and equalizing education, would-be academic freedom in the university, the maximal extension of culture—all these must be replaced by constraint, discipline [*Zucht*], and a process of selection under the direction of a guide, a leader or *Führer*, even a *grosse Führer*. It is only on this condition that the German spirit may be saved from its enemies—that spirit which is so "virile" in its "seriousness" [*männlich ernst*], so grave, hard, and hardy; that spirit which has been kept safe and sound since Luther, the "son of a miner," led the Reformation. The German university must be restored as a cultural institution, and to that end one must "renovate and resuscitate the purest ethical forces. And this must always be repeated to the student's credit. He was able to learn on the field of battle [1813] what he could learn least of all in the sphere of 'academic freedom': that one needs a grosse *Führer* and that all formation [*Bildung*] begins with obedience." The whole misfortune of today's students can be explained by the fact that they have not found a *Führer*. They remain *führerlos*, without a leader. "For I repeat it, my friends! All culture [*Bildung*] begins with the very opposite of that which is now so highly esteemed as 'academic freedom': *Bildung* begins with obedience [*Gehorsamkeit*], subordination [*Unterordnung*], discipline [*Zucht*] and subjection [*Dienstbarkeit*]. Just as great leaders [*die grossen Führer*] need followers, so those who are led need the leaders [*so bedürfen die zu Führenden der Führer*]—a certain reciprocal predisposition prevails in the order [*Ordnung*] of spirits here—yes, a kind of preestablished harmony. This eternal order . . ."

This preestablished ordinance or ordering of all eternity is precisely what the prevailing culture would attempt today to destroy or invert.

Doubtless it would be naive and crude simply to extract the word "*Führer*" from this passage and to let it resonate all by itself in its Hitlerian consonance, with the echo it received from the Nazi orchestration of the Nietzschean reference, as if this word had no other possible context. But it would be just as peremptory to deny that something is going on here that belongs to the *same* (the same what? the riddle remains), and which passes from the Nietzschean *Führer*, who is not merely a schoolmaster and master of doctrine, to the Hitlerian *Führer*, who also wanted to be taken for a spiritual and intellectual master, a guide in scholastic doctrine and practice, a teacher of regeneration. It would be just as peremptory and politically unaware as saying: Nietzsche never wanted that or thought that, he would have vomited it up, or he didn't intend it in that manner, he didn't hear it with that ear. Even if this were possibly true, one would be justified in finding very little of interest in such a hypothesis (one I am examining here from the angle of a very restricted corpus and whose other complications I set aside). I say this because, first of all, Nietzsche died as always *before* his name and therefore it is not a question of knowing what he would have thought, wanted, or done. Moreover, we have every reason to believe that in any case such things would have been quite complicated—the example of Heidegger gives us a fair amount to think about in this regard. Next, the effects or structure of a text are not reducible to its "truth," to the intended meaning of its presumed author, or even its supposedly unique and identifiable signatory. And even if Nazism, far from being the regeneration called for by these lectures of 1872, were only a symptom of the accelerated decomposition of European culture and society as diagnosed, it still remains to be explained how reactive degeneration could exploit the same language, the same words, the same utterances, the same rallying cries as the active forces to which it stands opposed. Of course, neither this phenomenon nor this specular ruse eluded Nietzsche.

The question that poses itself for us might take this form: Must there not be some powerful utterance-producing machine that programs the movements of the two opposing forces at once, and which couples, conjugates, or marries them in a given set, as life (does) death? (Here, all the difficulty comes down to the determination of such a set, which can be neither simply linguistic, nor simply historico-political, economic, ideological, psycho-phantasmatic, and so on. That is, no regional agency or tribunal has the power to arrest or set the limits on the set, not even that court of "last resort" belonging to philosophy or theory, which remain subsets of this set.) Neither of the two antagonistic forces can break with this powerful programming machine: it is their *destination;* they draw their points of origin and their resources from it; in it, they exchange utterances that are allowed to pass through the machine and into each other, carried along by family resemblances, however incompatible they may sometimes appear. Obviously, this "machine" is no longer a machine in the classic philosophical sense, because there is "life" in it or "life" takes part in it, and because it plays with the opposition life/ death. Nor would it be correct to say that this "program" is a program in the teleological or mechanistic sense of the term.

The "programming machine" that interests me here does not call only for decipherment but also for transformation—that is, a practical rewriting according to a theory–practice relationship which, if possible, would no longer be part of the program. It is not enough just to say this. Such a transformative rewriting of the vast program—if it were possible—would not be produced in books (I won't go back over what has so often been said elsewhere about general writing) or through readings, courses, or lectures on Nietzsche's writings, or those of Hitler and the Nazi ideologues of prewar times or today. Beyond all regional considerations (historical, poltico-economic, ideological, et cetera), Europe and not only Europe, this century and not only this century are at stake. And the stakes include the "present" in which we are, up to a certain point, and in which we take a position or take sides.

One can imagine the following objection: Careful! Nietzsche's utterances are not the same as those of the Nazi ideologues, and not only because the latter grossly caricaturize the former to the point of apishness. If one does more than extract certain short sequences, if one reconstitutes the entire syntax of the system with the subtle refinement of its articulations and its paradoxical reversals, et cetera, then one will clearly see that what passes elsewhere for the "same" utterance says exactly the opposite and corresponds instead to the inverse, to the reactive inversion of the very thing it mimes. Yet it would still be necessary to account for the possibility of this mimetic inversion and perversion. If one refuses the distinction between unconscious and deliberate programs as an absolute criterion, if one no longer considers only intent—whether conscious or not—when reading a text, then the law that makes the perverting simplification possible must lie in the structure of the text "remaining" (by which we will no longer understand the persisting substance of books, as in the expression *scripta manent*). Even if the intention of one of the signatories or shareholders in the huge "Nietzsche Corporation" had nothing to do with it, it cannot be entirely fortuitous that the discourse bearing his name in society, in accordance with civil laws and editorial norms, has served as a legitimating reference for ideologues. There is nothing absolutely contingent about the fact that the only political regimen to have *effectively* brandished his name as a major and official banner was Nazi.

I do not say this in order to suggest that this kind of "Nietzschean" politics is the only one conceivable for all eternity, nor that it corresponds to the best reading of the legacy, nor even that those who have not picked up this reference have produced a better reading of it. No. The future of the Nietzsche text is not closed. But if, within the still-open contours of an era, the only politics calling itself—proclaiming itself—Nietzschean will have been a Nazi one, then this is necessarily signficant and must be questioned in all of its consequences.

I am also not suggesting that we ought to reread "Nietzsche" and his great politics on the basis of what we know or think we know Nazism to be. I do not believe that we as yet know how to think what Nazism is. The task remains before us, and the political reading of the Nietzschean body or corpus is part of it. I would say the same is true for the Heideggerian, Marxian, or Freudian corpus, and for so many others as well.

In a word, has the "great" Nietzschean politics misfired or is it, rather, still to come in the wake of a seismic convulsion of which National Socialism or fascism will turn out to have been mere episodes?

I have kept a passage from *Ecce Homo* in reserve. It gives us to understand that we shall read the name of Nietzsche only when a great politics will have effectively entered into play. In the interim, so long as that name still has not been read, any question as to whether or not a given political sequence has a Nietzschean character would remain pointless. The name still has its whole future before it. Here is the passage:

I know my fate [*Ich kenne mein Los*]. One day my name will be associated with the memory of something monstrous [*Ungeheures*]— a crisis without equal on earth, the most profound collision of conscience [*Gewissens-Kollision*], a decision [*Entschiedung*] that was conjured up *against* everything that had been believed, demanded, hallowed so far. I am no man, I am dynamite.—Yet for all that, there is nothing in me of a founder of a religion—religions are affairs of the rabble; I find it necessary to wash my hands after I have come into contact with religious people.—I *want* no "believers"; I think I am too malicious to believe in myself; I never speak to masses—I have a terrible fear that one day I will be pronounced *holy:* you will guess why I publish this book *before;* it shall prevent people from doing mischief with me.

I do not want to be a holy man; sooner even a buffoon.—Perhaps I am a buffoon.—Yet in spite of that—or rather *not* in spite of it, because so far nobody has been more mendacious than holy men—the truth speaks out of me. . . .

The concept of politics will have merged entirely with a war of spirits; all power structures of the old society will have been exploded—all of them are based on lies: there will be wars the like of which have never yet been seen on earth. It is only beginning with me that the earth knows *great politics* [*grosse Politik*]. ("Why I Am a Destiny")

We are not, I believe, bound to decide. An interpretive decision does not have to draw a line between two intents or two political contents. Our interpretations will not be readings of a hermeneutic or exegetic sort, but rather political interventions in the political rewriting of the text and its destination. This is the way it has always been—and always in a singular manner—for example, ever since what is called the end of philosophy, and beginning with the textual indicator named "Hegel." This is no accident. It is an effect of the destinational structure of all so-called post-Hegelian texts. There can always be a Hegelianism of the left and a Hegelianism of the right, a Heideggerianism of the left and a Heideggerianism of the right, a Nietzscheanism of the right and a Nietzscheanism of the left, and even, let us not overlook it, a Marxism of the right and a Marxism of the left. The one can always be the other, the double of the other.

Is there anything "in" the Nietzschean corpus that could help us comprehend the double interpretation and the so-called perversion of the text? The Fifth Lecture tells us that there must be something _unheimlich_—uncanny—about the enforced repression [_Unterdrückung_] of the least degenerate needs. Why "_unheimlich_"? This is another form of the same question.

The ear is uncanny. Uncanny is what it is; double is what it can become; large or small is what it can make or let happen (as in laisser-faire, since the ear is the most tendered and most open organ, the one that, as Freud reminds us, the infant cannot close); large or small as well the manner in which one may offer or lend an ear. It is to her—this ear—that I myself will feign to address myself now in conclusion by speaking still more words in your ear, as promised, about your and my "academic freedom."

When the lectures appear to recommend linguistic discipline as a counter to the kind of "academic freedom" that leaves students and teachers free to their own thoughts or programs, it is not in order to set constraint over against freedom. Behind "academic freedom" one can discern the silhouette of a constraint which is all the more ferocious and implacable because it conceals and disguises itself in the form of laisser-faire. Through the said "academic freedom," it is the State that controls everything. The State: here we have the main defendant indicted in this trial. And Hegel, who is the thinker of the State, is also one of the principal proper names given to this guilty party. In fact, the autonomy of the university, as well as of its student and professor inhabitants, is a ruse of the State, "the most perfect ethical organism" (this is Nietzsche quoting Hegel). The State wants to attract docile and unquestioning functionaries to itself. It does so by means of strict controls and rigorous constraints which these functionaries believe they apply to themselves in an act of total auto-nomy. The lectures can thus be read as a modern critique of the cultural machinery of State and of the educational system that was, even in yesterday's industrial society, a fundamental part of the State apparatus. If today such an apparatus is on its way to being in part replaced by the media and in part associated with them, this only makes Nietzsche's critique of journalism—which he never dissociates from the educational apparatus—all the more strik-ing. No doubt he implements his critique from a point of view from that would make any Marxist analysis of this machinery, including the organizing concept of "ideology," appear as yet another symptom of degeneration or a new form of subjection to the Hegelian State. But one would have to look at things more closely: at the *several* Marxist concepts of State, at Nietzsche's opposition to socialism and democracy (in *The Twilight of the Idols,* he writes that "science is part of democ-racy"), at the opposition science/ideology, and so on. And one would have to look more closely at both sides. Elsewhere we shall pursue the development of this critique of the State in the fragments of the *Nachlass* and in *Zarathustra,* where, in the chapter "On the New Idol," one reads:

State? What is that? Well, then, open your ears to me. For now I shall speak to you about the death of peoples.

State is the name of the coldest of all cold monsters. Coldly it tells lies too; and this lie crawls out of its mouth: "I, the State, am the people." That is a lie! . . .

Confusion of tongues of good and evil: this sign I give you as the sign of the state. Verily, this sign signifies the will to death! Verily, it beckons to the preachers of death. . . .

"On earth there is nothing greater than I: the ordering finger of God am I"—thus roars the monster. And it is only the long-eared [asses] and shortsighted who sink to their knees! . . .

State I call it where all drink poison, the good and the wicked; state, where all lose themselves, the good and the wicked; state, where the slow suicide of all is called "life."

Not only is the State marked by the sign and the paternal figure of the dead, it also wants to pass itself off for the mother—that is, for life, the people, the womb of things them-selves. Elsewhere in *Zarathustra* ("On Great Events"), it is a hypocritical hound, which, like the Church, claims that its voice comes out of the "belly of reality."

The hypocritical hound whispers in your ear through his educational systems, which are actually acoustic or acroa-matic devices. Your ears grow larger and you turn into long-eared asses when, instead of listening with small, finely tuned ears and obeying the best master and the best of leaders, you think you are free and autonomous with respect to the State. You open wide the portals [_pavillons_] of your ears to admit the State, not knowing that it has already come under the control of reactive and degenerate forces. Having become all ears for this phonograph dog, you transform yourself into a high-fidelity receiver, and the ear—your ear which is also the ear of the other—begins to occupy in your body the disproportionate place of the "inverted cripple."

Is this our situation? Is it a question of the same ear, a borrowed ear, the one that you are lending me or that I lend myself in speaking? Or rather, do we hear, do we understand each other already with another ear?

The ear does not answer.

Who is listening to whom right here? Who was listening to Nietzsche when, in the Fifth Lecture, he lent his voice to the philosopher of his fiction in order to describe, for example, this situation?

Permit me, however, to measure this autonomy [_Selbstständigkeit_] of yours by the standard of this culture [_Bildung_], and to consider your university solely as a cultural establishment. If a foreigner desires to know something of our university system, he first of all asks emphatically: "How is the student connected with [_hängt zusammen_] the university?" We answer: "By the ear, as a listener." The foreigner is astonished: "Only by the ear?" he repeats. "Only by the ear," we again reply. The student listens. When he speaks, when he sees, when he walks, when he is in good company, when he takes up some branch of art: in short, when he _lives_, he is autonomous, i.e., not dependent upon the educational institution. Very often the student writes as he listens; and it is only at these moments that he hangs by the umbilical cord of the university [_an der Nabelschnur der Universität hängt_].

Dream this umbilicus: it has you by the ear. It is an ear, however, that dictates to you what you are writing at this moment when you write in the mode of what is called "taking notes." In fact the mother—the bad or false mother whom the teacher, as functionary of the State, can only simulate—dictates to you the very thing that passes through your ear and travels the length of the cord all the way down to your stenography. This writing links you, like a leash in the form of an umbilical cord, to the paternal belly of the State. Your pen is its pen, you hold its teleprinter like one of those Bic ballpoints attached by a little chain in the post office—and all its movements are induced by the body of the father figuring as alma mater. How an umbilical cord can create a link to this cold monster that is a dead father or the State—this is what is uncanny.

You must pay heed to the fact that the *omphalos* that Nietzsche compels you to envision resembles both an ear and a mouth. It has the invaginated folds and the involuted orificiality of both. Its center preserves itself at the bottom of an invisible, restless cavity that is sensitive to all waves which, whether or not they come from the outside, whether they are emitted or received, are always transmitted by this trajectory of obscure circumvolutions.

The person emitting the discourse you are in the process of teleprinting in this situation does not himself produce it; he barely emits it. He reads it. Just as you are ears that transcribe, the master is a mouth that reads, so that what you transcribe is, in sum, what he deciphers of a text that precedes him, and from which he is suspended by a similar umbilical cord. Here is what happens. I read: "It is only at these moments that he hangs by the umbilical cord of the university. He himself may choose what he will listen to; he is not bound to believe what he hears; he may close his ears if he does not care to hear. This is the acroamatic method of teaching." Abstraction itself: the ear can close itself off and contact can be suspended because the *omphalos* of a disjointed body ties it to a dissociated segment of the father. As for the professor, who is he? What does he do? Look, listen:

As for the professor, he speaks to these listening students. Whatever else he may think or do is cut off from the students' perception by an immense gap. The professor often reads when he is speaking. As a rule he prefers to have as many listeners as possible; in the worst of cases he makes do with just a few, and rarely with just one. One speaking mouth, with many ears, and half as many writing hands— there you have, to all appearances, the external academic apparatus [*äusserliche akademische Apparat*]; there you have the University culture machine [*Bildungsmaschine*] in action. The proprietor of the one mouth is severed from and independent of the owners of the many ears; and this double autonomy is enthusiastically called "academic freedom." What is more, by increasing this freedom a little, the one can speak more or less what he likes and the other may hear more or less what he wants to—except that, behind both of them, at a carefully calculated distance, stands the State, wearing the intent expression of an overseer, to remind the professors and students from time to time that *it* is the aim, the goal, the be-all and end-all [*Zweck, Ziel und Inbegriff*] of this curious speaking and hearing procedure.

End of quotation. I have just read and you have just heard a fragment of a discourse lent or cited by Nietzsche, placed in the mouth of an ironic philosopher ("the philosopher laughed, not altogether good-naturedly," before holding forth as has just been related). This philosopher is old. He has left the university, hardened and disappointed. He is not speaking at noon but after noon—at midnight. And he has just protested against the unexpected arrival of a flock, a horde, a swarm [*Schwarm*] of students. What do you have against students? they ask him. At first he does not answer; then he says:

"So, my friend, even at midnight, even on top of a lonely mountain, we shall not be alone; and you yourself are bringing a pack of mischief-making students along with you, although you well know that I am only too glad to put distance between me and *hoc genus omne*. I don't quite understand you, my distant friend . . . in this place where, in a memorable hour, I once came upon you as you sat in majestic solitude, and where we would earnestly deliberate with each other like knights of a new order. Let those who can understand us listen to us; but why should you bring with you a throng of people who don't understand us! I no longer recognize you, my distant friend!"

We did not think it proper to interrupt him during his disheartened lament: and when in melancholy he became silent, we did not dare to tell him how greatly this distrustful repudiation of students vexed us.

Omphalos

The temptation is strong for *all* of us to recognize *ourselves* on the program of this staged scene or in the pieces of this musical score. I would give a better demonstration of this if the academic time of a lecture did not forbid me to do so. Yes, to recognize *ourselves, all* of us, in these premises and within the walls of an institution whose collapse is heralded by the old midnight philosopher. ("Constructed upon clay founda- tions of the current *Gymnasien*-culture, on a crumbling groundwork, your edifice would prove to be askew and un- steady if a whirlwind were to swirl up.")

Yet, even if we were all to give in to the temptation of recognizing ourselves, and even if we could pursue the dem- onstration as far as possible, it would still be, a century later, all of us men—not all of us women—whom we recognize. For such is the profound complicity that links together the protagonists of this scene and such is the contract that con- trols everything, even their conflicts: woman, if I have read correctly, never appears at any point along the umbilical cord, either to study or to teach. She is the great "cripple," perhaps. No woman or trace of woman. And I do not make this remark in order to benefit from that supplement of seduction which today enters into all courtships or court- rooms. This vulgar procedure is part of what I propose to call "gynegogy."

No woman or trace of woman, if I have read correctly—save the mother, that's understood. But this is part of the system. The mother is the faceless figure of a *figurant*, an extra. She gives rise to all the figures by losing herself in the background of the scene like an anonymous persona. Everything comes back to her, beginning with life; everything addresses and des- tines itself to her. She survives on the condition of remaining at bottom.

ROUNDTABLE ON AUTOBIOGRAPHY

Translated by Peggy Kamuf

Rodolphe Gasché: *The Internal Border*

Yesterday, listening to "Otobiographies," we heard you, Jacques Derrida, proceed with a revalorization and a reevaluation of biography (a philosopher's; in this case, Nietzsche's) in relation to a written corpus. This procedure on your part might at first appear paradoxical, not to say disappointing. That is, if one were to listen to it with the wrong ear, then one could easily reinterpret your gesture as sketching out a return to certain academic positions—to psychobiography, for example—all the more so since, inevitably, you make use of the same language. Is it the same, however? As we will no doubt return to this question tomorrow during our discussion of translation, I will set it aside for the moment in order to inquire instead into how your approach to the problem of autobiography differs from traditional ones.

In the first place, autobiography, as you see it, is not to be in any way confused with the so-called life of the author, with the corpus of empirical accidents making up the life of an empirically real person. Rather, the biographical, insofar as it is autobiographical, cuts across both of the fields in question: the body of the work and the body of the real subject. The biographical is thus that internal border of work and life, a border on which texts are engendered. The status of the text— if it has one—is such that it derives from neither the one nor the other, from neither the inside nor the outside.

You say that *Ecce Homo* is an autobiographical text because in it the signatory recounts his life. You situate the lift-off point for this account of self to self in the case of *Ecce Homo* (and here I can't help thinking of the fantasy of auto-engendering in "The Case of Philippe," which Serge Leclaire analyzes in

Psychanalyser [1968]) in that leaf inserted between the preface and the text "properly speaking" which is neither the work nor the life of the author. As you put it, it is "between a title or a preface on the one hand, and the book to come on the other, between the title *Ecce Homo* and *Ecce Homo* 'itself.' " Heterogeneous to both the work and the life, this place of the "programming machine" engenders the text of which it is a part to the extent that it is a part larger than the whole.

My questions—which are actually a jumble of questions—will focus, then, on this localization of an interior borderline which, in principle, has to cut across the whole work. I will focus, that is, on that slice or part of the text which, as you say elsewhere, is not a part of the whole, is not a part at all.*

First question: What is the relation of the heterogeneous space of the text's engendering, perceptible in this leaf inserted between the title and *Ecce Homo* "properly speaking," to the "totality" of the text? Does this leaf have a privileged status precisely because it is empirically manifest? Does the empirical index of its being manifestly situated between the text "properly speaking" and the title give rise to some sort of privilege (to subvert, to engender, et cetera)? Or is the fact that it is situated and can thus be located and apprehended by the senses perhaps but one of the manifestations (that is, one of the possible translations) of the text's engendering which is at "work" throughout the totality of the text, an engendering which, in principle, necessarily escapes conversion into the empirical? In other words, what is the relation between the engendering place of the text and the empirical manifestations of this place in the text? What is the relation between the text's engendering border and the empirical given of the text? Can this relation still be thought of in terms of oppositions such as empirical/non-empirical? Does not your notion of text exclude, rather, any relation to the empirical? But in that case, what privileges the status of the inserted leaf?

n'est pas du tout, une tranche; n'est pas du tout une tranche. See below, pp. 104–05, for this use of "*tranche.*"—Tr.

Second question: You say that the heterogeneous space of the double programming in *Ecce Homo*, inasmuch as it is a space of eternal return and of the auto-affirmation of life, is one of auto-engendering and autobiography. In that space, Nietzsche in effect proposes to tell himself his life. The following question then arises: Do the heterogeneous spaces of a text's engendering necessarily have the structure of autobiography? Have they necessarily a relation to auto-biography? Or rather, would not auto-biography be but *one* of the possible names for this border of works and lives, but one of the figures (in the Heideggerian sense) that can be assumed by the question about what it is that cuts across these bodies (of the work, of the man) at their most intimate level? In short, then, my question comes down to integrating the status of autobiography as such.

Final question: What is the difference between autobiography as the name of the internal border of text, on the one hand, and the role played by autobiography in academic discourse on the other? To ask the same question in different terms: Do not both the affective *récit* and the affirmation of a concrete life set forth by such a *récit* uncover but the effect of the aporias or contradictions of a text's programming machine? Are they anything more than this effect? Do the reflectable aporias of an enterprise of auto-constitution and autobiography erect this machine at the border of the text they engender? Is the text anything other than the infinite unfolding of this machine? What limits the play of this machine? What determines that this play, which in principle is unlimited, takes the form of a finite life? Is it the empirical nature of a concrete life that limits this play, or are there rather constraints internal to the play that limit it?

Jacques Derrida: *Reply*

In order not to keep the floor too long and restrict the time for other questions, I will not try to give some answer based on principle to the very necessary and essential questions you have asked—because I have no such answers. Rather, I will try to specify why I cannot answer these questions and why their formulation is problematic for me. Without going back over the necessary and thoroughly convincing trajectory by which you led us to this formulation, I will skip right away to the first question, which concerns the relation between the text that you call "empirical" or "given" on the one hand, and, on the other, all of that which I tried to problematize yesterday around the value of the border. The problem is this: If one pursues carefully the questions that have been opened up here, then the very value of empiricalness, the very contours of an empirical text or any empirical entity, can perhaps no longer be determined. I can no longer say what an empirical text is, or the empirical given of a text. What I can do is refer to a certain number of conventions—precisely those conventions that sustain traditional or academic discourse, or even less traditional and less academic ones. When we employ such discourses, we think we know what a given text is—a text that we receive in the editorial form of an authenticated corpus, and so on. We also have a certain number of "empirical facts" about Nietzsche's life. Although there may be any number of debates on this subject, any number of disagreements about the content of these givens, the presupposition is, nevertheless, that one knows what one means by Nietzsche's "empirical" life. That is, one assumes that one knows what is at the organizing center of the debate. If one problematizes things as I tried to do yesterday, however, the opposition between, for example, the empirical and the non-empirical (but there are other names for this opposition) is precisely what becomes problematic. I then no longer know what this experience is that grounds the value of the empirical. This is the case whether one is speaking of Nietzsche's life or his corpus—his body, if you will—or the corpus called Nietzsche's works. As I tried to indicate yesterday, wherever the paradoxical problem of the border is posed, then the line that could separate an author's life from his work, for example, or which, within this life, could separate an essentialness or transcendentality from an empirical fact, or, yet again, within his work, an empirical fact from something that is not empirical—this very line itself becomes unclear. Its mark becomes divided; its unity, its identity becomes dislocated. When this identity is dislocated, then the problem of the *autos,* of the autobiographical, has to be totally redistributed.

Finally, if one gets around to wondering, as you did in your last question, about the status of the autobiographical, then one has to ask whether one will understand the autobiographical in terms of this internal border and all the rest, or instead rely on the standard concepts prevailing throughout tradition. Once again, one is faced with a division of the *autos,* of the autobiographical, but this doesn't mean that one has to dissolve the value of the autobiographical récit. Rather, one must restructure it otherwise on the basis of a project that is also biographical or thanatographical. And what name shall this redistribution be given in the "Nietzschean corpus" in general, in "Nietzsche's thought" in general, in "Nietzsche's signature," and so forth? It would all come down to setting Nietzsche's autobiography, or Nietzsche's autobiographical thought, on the back, so to speak, of some thought of the eternal return. That is, the autobiography is signed by something that arises out of the thought of the eternal return in Nietzsche.

Although I cannot undertake here an interpretation of the thought of the eternal return in Nietzsche, I will at least mention that the eternal return is selective. Rather than a repetition of the same, the return must be selective within a differential relation of forces. That which returns is the constant affirmation, the "yes, yes" on which I insisted yesterday. That which signs here is in the form of a return, which is to say it has the form of something that cannot be simple. It is a selective return without negativity, or which reduces negativity through affirmation, through alliance or marriage [*hymen*], that is, through an affirmation that is also binding on the other or that enters into a pact with itself as other. The difficulty and thus the risk with the gesture I'm sketching out here is that it will, once again, relate the autobiographical signature (which one always expects to be idiomatic, singular, subject to chance, and so forth) to something as essential as the eternal return. This might lead one to think that once again something empirical, individual, et cetera, is going to be related to an essential thought—that of the eternal return. However, I believe this risk can be avoided if, precisely, one thinks in terms of what Nietzsche has perhaps made available to thought and which he calls the eternal return. The point is that the eternal return is not a new metaphysics of time or of the totality of being, et cetera, on whose ground Nietzsche's autobiographical signature would come to stand like an empirical fact on a great ontological structure. (Here, one would have to take up again the Heideggerian interpretations of the eternal return and perhaps problematize them.) The eternal return always involves differences of forces that perhaps cannot be thought in terms of being, of the pair essence–existence, or any of the great metaphysical structures to which Heidegger would like to relate them. As soon as it crosses with the motif of the eternal return, then the individual signature, or, if you like, the signature of a proper name, is no longer simply an empirical fact grounded in something other than itself. Given the many difficulties in translating what I am trying to get hold of, I would say that here perhaps may be found not the answer but the enigma to which Nietzsche refers when he speaks of his identity, his genealogy, and so on.

Christie V. McDonald: *From One Genre to the Other*

What I have to say concerns the question of genre, specifically the one that is traditionally or commonly called autobiography and is itself, in principle, the subject of our discussion today. If one may say that genres demonstrate in a particular way what constitutes the society or institution to which they belong, then it follows that a given society chooses and codifies those acts that correspond to its dominant ideology. You already alluded to this problem when you said that an institution is more tolerant of certain explicitly ideological expressions (even those having a revolutionary aim) than it is of a conception of writing such as the one practiced, for example, in your deconstructive texts. Perhaps it is possible to approach this question through the implicit slippage in your title "Otobiographies," that is, the passage from _auto_biography to _oto_biography, reversing the chronological order from yesterday to this afternoon.

Let me explain this by means of a certain number of detours. It seems to me that the synchronic consideration of genre tends to make apparent the particular elements structuring so-called literary form. That is, characteristics and techniques of a genre can be described by those functions that point to the generic system. But the question then arises: How is one to place a specific text within a diachronic series, which presupposes both variable and invariable factors (a tradition, an order, and conventions that degenerate before regenerating themselves in some other way)? Here I am thinking less of the external history of what has been called autobiography (whether one takes it back to Rousseau, Saint Augustine, or other writers) than of the critical act that, in its interpretive relation to the text, imposes a meaning on it. In this latter context, could one say that the principle of a traditional genre is fundamentally that of an order which, even though it does not remain fixed, makes possible the production of meaning and gives rise to hermeneutic discourse as meaningful discourse?

As for the so-called modern genres, it has been observed (by T. Todorov in _Les Genres du discours_ [1978]) that one can detect two divergent tendencies in a writer like Blanchot. First, the paradoxical notion of the singular book as itself the ultimate genre, where each work does not simply derive from a genre but also interrogates, through its very particularity, the very status of literature. The second tendency is a movement to replace past genres (such as the story, dialogue, or diary) with others that transgress or surpass them. It seems to me that this movement closely parallels your own (in "Living On: Borderlines," for example). Now, the genre we are discussing—autobiography—marks the confusion between the notion of the author and that of the person, the confusion that Rodolphe Gasché has just evoked and which Nietzsche seems to refuse in *Ecce Homo*. In this, Nietzsche with you, and you together with Nietzsche, pose the problem of the text—of its beginning and its origin—in terms of a relation between the one who signs (the author) and the one who reads or, as you put it yesterday, who hears.

My question has two parts. First of all, can it be that here— between two texts (*Ecce Homo* and *On the Future of Our Educational Institutions*) and two terms (autobiography and otobiography), and despite the anachronistic order—one encounters one of those passages from the *critical*, based on transportable univocality and formalizable polysemia, to the *deconstructive*? In other words, is it here that we find a passage to that which overflows in the direction of dissemination and seems to concern problems of political and institutional order in the university? If so, is it possible to link the deconstructive to any particular ideological content (of teaching in the institution)? Whether the power struggle be political, religious, economic, or technical, how is one to formulate it in writing when, at a certain level, writing is itself an interpretation of power? What does one do with the transmission of this power which is the very decipherment of the text?

Second, as I decided to open with the question of the autobiographical genre, that place of a contract signed by the author, I would like to relate the two parts of my question to the pronoun "I," which is not only the addresser but the addressee, the one for whom one always writes, and only in his/her absence. At the beginning of *Speech and Phenomena,* you placed this passage from Edmund Husserl in exergue: "When we read the word 'I' without knowing who wrote it, it is perhaps not meaningless, but it is at least estranged from its normal meaning." You then followed, it seems to me, a program explicitly laid out in a later text (*Pas*), where you say that "in order to accede to another text, another's text, one must assume, in a certain very determined manner, the fault, the weakness, not avoiding what the other will have managed to avoid, so as to make him/her appear in this withdrawing and in this redrawing." You have underlined not only the anonymity of the *written I* [*je écrit*] but also the inappropriateness of the *I write* [*j'écris*] as the "normal situation." My question: In the reading or readings that remain to be done of Nietzsche by this deciphering ear, and without letting oneself get caught in the trap of what you have called gynegogy, does the "I" have a gender [*genre*]?*

Jacques Derrida: *Reply*

I should not have to reply right away to such fully elaborated and serious questions—and by improvising no less. Our agreement for this exchange is that I should try to improvise a response even when I am not sure that I can do so adequately. Well, I am sure that in a few sentences I will not be able to meet the demands of a question whose elaborations and presuppositions are of such a vast scope. Nevertheless, I'll take my chances with an answer.

First of all, as concerns that obviously deliberate transformation of *auto* into *oto*, which has been reversed in a chiasmatic fashion today: Notice that the institution has calculated this reversal so precisely that today we find ourselves in the Great Pavilion, whereas yesterday we were somewhere else.† The play that accompanies this transformation would be of no interest if it were not itself carried along by a necessity which I tried, to a certain degree, to make apparent yesterday. If today I am trying to reformulate it, it is because this necessity requires that we pass by way of the ear—the ear involved in any autobiographical discourse that is still at the stage of hearing oneself speak. (That is: I am telling myself my story, as Nietzsche said, here is the story that I am telling myself; and that means I hear myself speak.) I speak myself to myself in a certain manner, and my ear is thus immediately plugged into

Genre also means "gender."—Tr.

†As in the pavilion of the ear, the visible part of the aural apparatus.—Tr.

my discourse and my writing. But the necessity of passing onto and by way of the ear is not just this. Nor is it just the necessity of the labyrinth motif which, in Nietzsche, plays an altogether decisive role with the figures of Ariadne and Dionysus. To be more precise, it is, in the context that interested me yesterday, *the difference in the ear*. First of all, the difference in the ear is, clearly, the difference in the size of ears. There are smaller or larger ears. The larger the ear, the more it is bent toward the pavilion, if you will, and the more undifferentiated it is, the more finesse it lacks in its attention to difference.

Nietzsche prides himself on having small ears (by implication, keen ears). A keen ear is an ear with keen hearing, an ear that perceives differences, those differences to which he was very attentive. And precisely to perceive differences is to pass on the distinction between apparently similar things. Think of all that was said yesterday about political discourses and about stereotypes that seem to resemble each other. Here, precisely, is where the keen ear must be able to distinguish the active from the reactive, the affirmative from the negative, even though apparently they are the same thing: to decide with a keen ear in order to perceive differences and in order to seduce (as when Nietzsche says in passing, "I have small ears and this is of no small interest to women"). The ear is not only an auditory organ; it is also a visible organ of the body.

The most important thing about the ear's difference, which I have yet to remark, is that the signature becomes effective—performed and performing—not at the moment it apparently takes place, but only later, when ears will have managed to receive the message. In some way the signature will take place on the addressee's side, that is, on the side of him or her whose ear will be keen enough to hear my name, for example, or to understand my signature, that with which I sign. According to the logic that I tried to reconstitute yesterday, Nietzsche's signature does not take place when he writes. He says clearly that it will take place posthumously, pursuant to the infinite line of credit he has opened for himself, when the other comes to sign with him, to join with him in alliance and, in order to do so, to hear and understand him. To hear him, one must have a keen ear. In other words, to abbreviate my remarks in a very lapidary fashion, it is the ear of the other that signs. The ear of the other says me to me and constitutes the *autos* of my autobiography. When, much later, the other will have perceived with a keen-enough ear what I will have addressed or destined to him or her, then my signature will have taken place. Here one may derive the political import of this structure and of this signature in which the addressee signs with his/her ear, an organ for perceiving difference. As regards Nietzsche, for example, it is we who have to honor his signature by interpreting his message and his legacy politically. On this condition, the signature contract and the autobiography will take place. It is rather paradoxical to think of an autobiography whose signature is entrusted to the other, one who comes along so late and is so unknown. But it is not Nietzche's originality that has put us in this situation. Every text answers to this structure. It is the structure of textuality in general. A text is signed only much later by the other. And this testamentary structure doesn't befall a text as if by accident, but constructs it. This is how a text always comes about.

I make a connection here to one of the other motifs in your question. Within the university—an institution that institutes above all the transmission of what has been inherited, the conservation and interpretation of the archive, and so on—we are constantly obliged to make the gesture that consists in honoring, so to speak, the other's signature. In the terms of this context, the gesture consists in hearing, while we speak and as acutely as possible, Nietzsche's voice. But this does not mean that one simply receives it. To hear and understand it, one must also produce it, because, like his voice, Nietzsche's signature awaits its own form, its own event. This event is entrusted to us. Politically *and* historically (not just politically, unless one understands "politically" in the broadest sense of the word), it is we who have been entrusted with the responsibility of the signature of the other's text which we have inherited. Nor is it just Nietzsche's text or Nietzsche's signature that we are responsible for, since the borderless text itself is involved along with the signature and also since, given the questions we have asked about the border, the signature is not only a word or a proper name at the end of a text, but the operation as a whole, the text as a whole, the whole of the active interpretation which has left a trace or a remainder. It is in this respect that we have a political responsibility. As regards such responsibility, I have no answer of a general sort in the form of a watchword. I have to be satisfied—and perhaps it's no small matter—with defining the general space of this responsibility.

The most difficult question came at the end of your remarks. It concerns the sexual gender (and not simply the literary genre) of the "I" whose grammatical form is indeterminate, at least in the languages we are using here. When I say "I" or "*je*," "you" or "*vous*," the grammatico-sexual mark is not perceptible or audible. This poses many different problems from a linguistic standpoint. One may encounter the problem of translation, which we are going to address specifically tomorrow. I will therefore set this aspect aside. But going a step beyond, if you will, the logico-grammatical aspect of the problem, one finds that the question of the ear or the addressee returns. It concerns the other to whom, at bottom, I entrust my signature. The question is whether the difference constituting the other as other has, a priori, to be marked sexually. I don't know. When I say "I don't know," I mean that in order to ask the question as I have posed it, one must presuppose that the addresser himself or herself is determined before the other's signature, that the sex of the addresser is itself determined before the other assumes responsibility for the signature. Well, nothing seems less certain to me. I will go so far as to risk this hypothesis: The sex of the addresser awaits its determination by or from the other. It is the other who will perhaps decide who I am—man or woman. Nor is this decided once and for all. It may go one way one time and another way another time. What is more, if there is a multitude of sexes (because there are perhaps more than two) which sign differently, then I will have to assume (*I*—or rather whoever says *I*—will have to assume) this polysexuality. This is what I risk, of course, but I

would like to
aps a certain
ch you made
I am, a certain
r *und der,* a
not be able to
it with an ear
e living femi-
r who is dead
eover, outlive
g on, and this
val is my life
ame, in other
death, of my
re, one reads:
an allo- and

nt thanatogra-
y beginning of
ion, it would
n's "value has
peaking of the
c is a theory of
, the thanatog-
f resurrection,
permits resur-
ences), would
s is what does
oes sign)? One
raphy and the
always some-
ot be sublated

we received yesterday from
lf says, I am two, my father
its consequences, one finds
uality among others. It com-
plurality. His mother and his
who are also life and death,
therefore many other things.
id he has not only inherited
a. He also writes *for them,* a
esterday. (I even wonder if I
which said that.) The point
as it is manifested in this
il. But, inasmuch as it sur-
addressee in the phantasm,
e because he writes also for
s for his father, if therefore,
are yet to live but also for
have gone before us, then
going to end by going very
so for the dead. Obviously,
in, and perhaps we will be
ey are not so difficult if one
yesterday about the proper
t to be confused with the
exists and is meant to exist
us, every name is the name
someone whom it can do
own writing is names or if
es, then one writes also for
d in general, as Jean Genet
e "I write for the dead" or
d." Rather, one writes for a
ps in every text there is a
he singular figure of death
ch signs. Now, if the other
at has a certain number of

n. It was too difficult.

Eugenio Donato: *A Third Logic*

What I have to say is not a question. Instead,
point up several landmarks that suggest per
path. I'll begin by reading the passage to wh
allusion just a moment ago. "There, this is who
masculine and a certain feminine. *Ich bin d*
phrase which means all these things. You will
hear and understand my name unless you hear
attuned to the name of the dead man and th
nine—the double and divided name of the fathe
and the mother who is living on, who will, mo
me long enough to bury me. The mother is livi
living on is the name of the mother. This sur
whose shores she overflows. And my father's
words my patronym? That is the name of m
dead life." Somewhat further on in the lect
"There is here a differance of autobiography
thanatography."

What I would like to extricate are the differe
phies or scenarios of thanatography. At the ve
your work, you informed us that, in some fas
always be a question of a thanatography. The si
the structure of a testament," you said. And, s
speculative dialectic, you also said, "The dialect
death." First of all, with respect to thanatograph
raphy of the dialectic, which is a thanatography
of the resuscitated dead, of the speculation tha
rection (from which there follow certain conseq
one be justified in saying, for example, that th
not sign (as opposed to Nietzsche, the one who
may find a relation between this first thanato
first logic of deconstruction in which there wa
thing of the dead that remained and that could
by the dialectical operation.

At the other end of your work, you proposed a completely different logic which, in fact, totally shattered this dialectical movement. I am referring to the crypt. Is the dialectic of the crypt a different logic from the one you proposed yesterday, insofar as the crypt's logic puts in play the living dead and does not permit any sublation of the cadaver? I heard yesterday's text as a third logic in this thanatology. The logic of my father the dead, my mother the living, my father the forever dead, my mother the forever living would be a logic that leads to an irreducible doubleness. You say, moreover, that it would lead to a split dialectic of the negative. Here, for example, one might note the following passage: "As a 'living' father, he was already only the memory of life, of an already prior life. Elsewhere, I have related this elementary kinship structure (of a dead or rather absent father, already absent to himself, and of the mother living above and after all, living on long enough to bury the one she has brought into the world, an ageless virgin inaccessible to all ages) to a logic of the death knell [*glas*] and of *obsequence*." Later you add, "The contradiction of the 'double' thus goes beyond whatever declining negativity might accompany a dialectical opposition." Speaking in very general terms, I see here a trajectory that sets out from Nietzsche as a reader of Hegel in relation to the problem of the dialectic. However, in this Nietzsche reader-of-Hegel, I also read an autobiographical element: Derrida rereading *Of Grammatology* today. And in Nietzsche's thanatography, I see the necessity of the signature, the necessary inability to assume and sublate in the autobiography the limit-position of the living dead, that is to say, of the crypt.

Based on what you have written recently on Freud and on psychoanalysis, one can say that this logic of the living dead makes the identification of the Freudian Oedipus absolutely impossible. That is, the father who is always dead and the mother who is always living would constitute in fact a movement that deconstructs the psychoanalytic Oedipus, a movement that would eventually reduce Freud to Hegel.

Jacques Derrida: *Reply*

These are very, very difficult questions which naturally concern me and seem to me altogether necessary, although once again it is going to be hard for me to survey the enormous field that you have marked off. To begin with what I can best grasp immediately, I'll recall what you said about Hegel and Nietzsche: the former would be the one who did not sign and the other the one who signs Nietzsche. In effect, that appears to be the case. In *Glas,* I said that Hegel seemed not to sign; and yesterday I began by saying Nietzsche is someone who wanted to sign. That appears to be the case. Hegel presents himself as a philosopher or a thinker, someone who constantly tells you that his empirical signature—the signature of the individual named Hegel—is secondary. His signature, that is, pales in the face of the truth, which speaks through his mouth, which is produced in his text, which constructs the system it constructs. This system is the teleological outcome of all of Western experience, so that in the end Hegel, the individual, is nothing but an empirical shell which can fall away without subtracting from the truth or from the history of meaning. As a philosopher and as a teacher, he seems to be saying basically that not only is it possible for his signature and his proper name to disappear without a loss, to fall outside of the system, but that this is even necessary in his own system because it will prove the truth and the autonomy of that system. Thus, my exclusion from what I am saying—the exclusion of my signature from the text produced through me—is absolutely essential and necessary if my discourse is to be a philosophical, ontological one. It appears, then, that Hegel did not sign. Inversely, it appears that Nietzsche signs and signs more than once. He is someone who writes his autobiography, recalls his name, his genealogy, and so forth. Yet, in fact, Hegel signs just as clearly. One could show, as I have tried to do elsewhere, in what way it was difficult to dispense with the name of Hegel in his work, to withold its inscription—call it personal or biographical—from his work. It implies a reelaboration of the whole problematic of the biographical within philosophy. Inversely, Nietzsche has great trouble signing. He wants to sign but he is obliged to defer his signature, to entrust it to something like the eternal return which will not sign just once by stating an identity. Rather, it will sign the strongest indefinitely, it will select the strongest, and finally it will sign only in the form of the difference of forces and qualities. It will not sign in the form of the patronym. Thus, Nietzsche has a lot of trouble signing. He doesn't complain about it, but in any case he didn't sign in the common sense of the term. He defers his signature.

The question concerning the crypt is much more difficult because, in order to reconstitute this problematic carefully, one would have to refer once more to the psychoanalytic theory of the crypt elaborated by the French psychoanalysts Nicolas Abraham and Maria Torok [_Le Verbier de l'Homme aux loups_ (1976); _L'Ecorce et le noyau_ (1978)]. To review very quickly, the alternative topical description they have proposed came out of their work reelaborating the Freudian theory of melancholia and mourning. They have proposed the concept of the crypt. Now, what is the crypt in this instance? It is that which is constituted as a crypt in the body for the dead object in a case of unsuccessful mourning, mourning that has not been brought to a normal conclusion. The metaphor of the crypt returns insistently. Not having been taken back inside the self, digested, assimilated as in all "normal" mourning, the dead object remains like a living dead abscessed in a specific spot in the ego. It has its place, just like a crypt in a cemetery or temple, surrounded by walls and all the rest. The dead object is incorporated in this crypt—the term "incorporated" signaling precisely that one has failed to digest or assimilate it totally, so that it remains there, forming a pocket in the mourning body. The incorporated dead, which one has not really managed to take upon oneself, continues to lodge there

like something other and to ventrilocate through the "living."
The living dead, to which Eugenio Donato made allusion, is
the one who is enclosed in the crypt. For instance, I lose a
loved one, I fail to do what Freud calls the normal work of
mourning, with the result that the dead person continues to
inhabit me, but as a stranger. By contrast, in normal mourning,
if such a thing exists, I take the dead upon myself, I digest it,
assimilate it, idealize it, and interiorize it in the Hegelian
sense of the term. This is what Hegel calls interiorization
which is at the same time memorization—an interiorizing memorization (*Erinnerung*) which is idealizing as well. In the work
of mourning, the dead other (it may be an object, an animal, or
some other living thing) is taken into me: I kill it and remember it. But since it is an *Erinnerung*, I interiorize it totally and
it is no longer other. Whereas in unsuccessful mourning, this
Erinnerung goes only so far and then stops. What Abraham
and Torok call introjection (another term for interiorization)
reaches its limit: incorporation marks the limit of introjection.
I cannot manage to interiorize the dead other so I keep it in
me, as a persecutor perhaps, a living dead.

My review of this theorization is obviously too succinct. As
for the interpretation of Nietzsche that I proposed yesterday, is
it in any way foreign to this theorization? Is not the way in
which Nietzsche relates himself to his father and mother, for
example, something else? I don't know. Obviously when
Nietzsche says, "I am at once the dead man and the living
woman," he says to himself, I am both of them. He has in him
some living dead; he is also then this couple's crypt (since his
father and mother are not two but one couple). He has in him
this living-dead couple, and this general situation could open
onto a general space within which to ask the question of
Nietzsche's crypt. Perhaps. Through his father and his mother,
he may be both pointing to and hiding some other, far more
determinate ghost. I'm not prepared to analyze Nietzsche's
ghost right now, but such an analysis could be attempted or
situated in the general space where he says: "I am my father
and my mother; I am my dead father and my living mother. I

am their crypt and they both speak to me. They both speak in me so whatever I say, they address it to each other."

I don't know if you can tell from this very scanty summary, but the analysis of a crypt can be done only according to procedures that are far from classical in psychoanalysis. The forms of the "analytic situation," and even the process of transference and so on, are unsettled by Abraham's and Torok's theory about the crypt. When it's a text that one is trying to decipher or decrypt using these concepts and these motifs, or when one is looking for a ghost or a crypt in a text, then things get still more difficult, or let us say more novel. I say a ghost _and_ a crypt: actually the theory of the "ghost" is not exactly the theory of the "crypt." It's even more complicated. Although it's also connected to the crypt, the ghost is more precisely the effect of another's crypt in my unconscious.

Now, as for Nietzsche being a reader of Hegel: it's a standard topic, of course. Nietzsche is a reader and a major critic of Hegel. All of Nietzsche's affirmations can be interpreted as anti-Hegelian affirmations. Well, obviously, as is always the case when one has a great adversary—and Hegel is Nietzsche's great adversary, isn't he?—there will be moments when the adversaries greatly resemble each other. It would be easy to show that there is a dialectic, a Hegelianism in Nietzsche.

Patrick Mahony: _Play, Work, and Beyond_

My first question concerns the influence of autobiography on theoretical concepts.

According to the German romantic poet Friedrich Schiller, man is thoroughly human only when he gives himself over to the activity of play. In parallel with this provocative notion, I will place the similar position of Donald Winnicott, the British psychoanalyst, who writes:

It is in playing and only in playing that the individual child or adult is able to be creative and to use the whole personality, and it is only in being creative that the individual discovers the self. (Bound up with this is the fact that only in playing is communication possible.) . . . In terms of free association . . . the patient on the couch or the child patient among the toys on the floor must be allowed to communicate a succession of ideas, thoughts, impulses, sensations that are not linked except in some way that is neurological or physiological and perhaps beyond detection. . . . Perhaps it is to be accepted that there are patients who at times need the therapist to note the nonsense that belongs to the state of the individual at rest without the need even for the patient to communicate this nonsense, that is to say, without the need for the patient to organize nonsense. (*Playing and Reality*, pp. 54–56)

Winnicott's ready acceptance of the nonsense of free association situates him at a certain distance from the principal approach of the orthodox psychoanalysts, such as Freud, [Sándor] Ferenczi, and [Rudolph] Loewenstein, who insisted not only that the patient communicate freely but that free association be comprehensible. Actually, Freud's reservations with regard to free play come to the fore at this point. One day he was asked what a normal person has to do to keep in good health, and he replied simply: "Love and work" ([Erik] Erikson, *Identity, Youth and Crisis* [1968]). He did not include "play." In this way, Freud departs from Schiller and Winnicott. A pertinent remark in this regard is Freud's pronounced distaste for music. What is more, when one considers certain of his psychoanalytic concepts, one notices that several different phenomena are repeatedly referred to in terms of work rather than play: *Durcharbeitung* (working through), *psychische Verarbeitung* (psychical working out), *sekundäre Bearbeitung* (secondary elaboration), *Traumarbeit* (dream work), *Trauerarbeit* (mourning work), *Witzarbeit* (joke work).

Now, play has an enormously important place in your work, play which is nonetheless serious at the same time. Following the quotations I am going to read, I cannot help thinking that Freud's superego, which, as he says, casts a shadow over the ego, must have incited him to work in different terms.

1. "One could call *play* the absence of the transcendental signified as limitlessness of play, that is to say as the destruc-

tion of onto-theology and the metaphysics of presence. . . . Here one must think of writing as the play within language" (*Of Grammatology,* p. 50);

2. "The presence–absence of the trace, which one should not even call its ambiguity but rather its play . . ." (*ibid.,* p. 71);

3. "I try to respect as rigorously as possible the internal play of philosophemes or epistememes by making them slide—without mistreating them—to the point of their non-pertinence, their exhaustion, their closure" (*Positions,* p. 6).

Finally, there is your watchword from *Glas:* "Let the net float, the infinitely twisted and crafty play of knots."

I would like to hear you comment on what is an obvious difference between Winnicott and Freud and on how you situate yourself in relation to this difference.

After having carefully studied Freud's *Beyond the Pleasure Principle* in the original language as well as various commentaries on it, I can justly say that I consider the best reading of it to be your "Freud's Legacy" ["Legs de Freud"]. I have studied your text three times, and each time I better appreciate the precise description it gives of the second chapter of Freud's treatise. The chapter is read as a performative discourse with a mimetic structure and also as an auto-hetero-bio-thanatography which gives "a more or less vivid description of Freud's own writing, his manner of writing what he writes" (p. 96).

Whatever one's approach to autobiography—literary, philosophical, et cetera—one must pay constant attention to the unlimited factor of the repetition compulsion. You have essentially taken up this idea again in "Freud's Legacy," and I would like to explore it further with you. The best way to do so is to use the specific example you have chosen.

Elsewhere in Freud's production, one may point to an impressive number of major texts that consist of seven chapters: *The Interpretation of Dreams; Jokes and Their Relation to the Unconscious;* "The Question of Lay Analysis," "The Unconscious," and *New Introductory Lectures on Psycho-Analysis.*

The first two parts of *Three Essays on the Theory of Sexuality* each has seven sections, as does Freud's favorite text, part four of *Totem and Taboo*. Also notice that there are twenty-eight lectures in the *Introduction to Psycho-Analysis*—a multiple of seven. The friendship between Freud and his great friend Wilhelm Fliess lasted about fourteen years, that between Freud and Jung almost seven years. The famous Secret Committee which guided the psychoanalytic movement consisted of seven members each of whom wore a ring. Finally, the city of Rome, with its seven hills, was so off-limits for Freud that for several years he was unable to visit it, and, after he finally did so, he went there a total of seven times.

Prompted by your theories about textuality, decentering, and *mise en abîme*,* I would now like to bring to your attention a certain series of traces in Freud's work. More precisely, I think we may gain new autobiographical insight if we compare Freud's treatise on death from 1920 to the most famous of all dreams in the psychoanalytic literature. I am referring to the so-called Irma dream which Freud had twenty-five years earlier and which, for all we know, revealed to him, through the analysis he made of it, the secret of dreams in general. I want to emphasize two references in the dream: first, the patient, Irma, a direct reference to Freud's wife who was at that time pregnant with their daughter Anna; second, the very important reference to the nose. I will explain the latter first.

The counterpart to Freud's autoanalysis was Fliess's autotherapy or his operations on the nose. Earlier, the two of them had begun, on Fliess's suggestion, to keep daily records of their personal observations. These personal observations were organized around the nasal-reflex neurosis, a clinical category proposed by Fliess, an otorhinolaryngologist, who was represented in the dream by Otto. (Hence, Freud's autoanalysis was

*The abyssal effect by which a represented object, scene, et cetera, already figures within the frame of the representation, thus precluding the idea of any original moment or space that is outside the frame. It would be the effect, for example, of a painting of a gallery wall on which hung the painting of the gallery wall.—Tr.

likewise an otoanalysis, and the dream took the form of an otography.) The nose was supposed to be the source of the greatest variey of symptoms which might appear anywhere in the body—from migraines to back pains—all of which could be relieved by nasal surgery and the nasal administration of cocaine. Next, Fliess set out the principle of female cycles of twenty-eight days and male cycles of twenty-three days, and linked the two in order to determine the days of a person's birth and death. Finally, he established a strict relation between the morphology and functioning of the nose, on the one hand, and of the genitalia, on the other. As we know, Freud was delighted with this diagram which allowed one to glimpse the possibility of a biological basis for psychoanalysis as well as an effective solution to the problem of birth control.

Now, in the Irma dream, Sigmund (*Sieg Mund*: victory mouth) looks into Irma's mouth and throat as an otorhinolaryngologist would do (thus the dream is a laryngography). At first Sigmund feels Irma's case has defeated him. Then, in pursuit of victory, he begins to accuse his friend Otto (Fliess) of having used a dirty syringe to give Irma, who is pregnant, a shot of trimethylamin. But here, let us listen to Freud's own association on his dream: "I began to guess why the formula for trimethylamin had been so prominent in the dream. So many important subjects converged upon that one word. Trimethylamin was an allusion not only to the immensely powerful factor of sexuality, but also to [Fliess] . . . who had a special knowledge of the consequences of affections of the nose and its accessory cavities" (*Standard Edition*, 4:117).

For our part, when we transcribe the whole of the important chemical formula to which Freud merely alludes, we notice that the symbol for nitrogen occurs as a heteroatom which is not in brackets. The letter, the chemical sign for nitrogen, in its graphic relation, is the same as the first consonant of the word nose (*Nase*) while it also represents a sound that is inevitably performed nasally. (The dream is thus a rhinography.) We see that the *n* signifies more than this when we recall that

Freud considered his governess (*Kinderfrau*) very important even though he referred to her by the altogether inappropriate term "nurse" (*Amme*). By his own avowal, it was she who was the "original author" of his neurosis, who talked to him about hell and initiated him into sexual matters.

It is only natural to suppose that she played an important role in his infantile masturbation. Yet Freud was extremely reserved on this subject, and no reference to it appears in his autobiographical *Interpretation of Dreams*. In fact, at one point Freud totally denies that the child has any sexuality, a striking contradiction which Jung did not fail to notice. All the same, several interesting facts turn up on this subject in Freud's manuscript notes on the Rat Man case. Although Freud uses both German words for masturbation—*Masturbation* and *Onanie*—he had the habit of abbreviating this reference with the capital initial. This condensation is quite significant as a compromise formation, since it remains an iconic symbol even as it refers to the repressed Nanny. Thus the *O* is a trace of his Nanny, of infantile masturbation, and of Fliess's nasal theories. I said "trace," but the term Freud used was either *Zeichen* [sign] or *Spur* [scent]—the latter, with its olfactory reference, frequently occurs in Freud's texts.

What is more, although Freud had broken off relations with Fliess in 1900, about ten years later, in 1910, traces—*Spuren*—of Fliess still remained with Freud. In that year, when the father and sons of the psychoanalytic primal horde founded the International Psychoanalytic Association, there were disagreements with [Wilhelm] Stekel and [Viktor] Tausk, the ghosts of Fliess. In the same year, Freud wrote his studies of Leonardo da Vinci and [Daniel Paul] Schreber, in each case a choice motivated by the homosexual elements which Freud linked to Fliess. During the same year, he refused to go to Innsbruck, giving as his only reason that it was there that he had had one of his first arguments with Fliess. More important, it was the year in which the Wolf Man began four years of treatment with Freud. Here, there are three facts to consider: first of all, when the Wolf Man returned to take up his treatment with Freud once more, his adolescent anxieties about his nose came out again; second, as [James] Strachey says (S.E., 17:6), the most important clinical discovery in the Wolf Man case was the determining role that the patient's primary feminine impulses played in his neurosis; third, during the second analysis of the Wolf Man, Freud was working on a draft of *Beyond the Pleasure Principle* and he felt compelled to voice certain doubts about Fliess's theory of feminine and masculine cycles.

Let's return now to the Irma dream in order to pick up another thread that can be subtly woven into the textual pattern of *Beyond the Pleasure Principle*. Recall that at the time of the dream, Freud's wife was pregnant with their daughter Anna, named after Anna Hammerschlag, a childless woman and the same Anna Hammerschlag represented by Irma, who is also identified with Freud's wife. Thus, thanks to the identification between mother and fetus, there is no metonymy, no difference between container and contained, inside and outside. Similarly, the subject Anna resists being contained by her father's *analysis*. As a palindrome, Anna's name is reversible: its beginning is identical to its end. What is more, Anna resembles *Amme* and *Onanie*, and there is thus another link with Fliess. We also know that if the child had been a boy, he would have been given Fliess's first name, Wilhelm. As impossible as it seems, Freud later tried to *analyze* his daughter. This analysis was carried out between 1918 and 1921, a period which includes the writing of *Beyond the Pleasure Principle*. In fact, one ought to understand Anna's later book *The Ego and the Mechanisms of Defense* (1936) in terms of a deferred motivation whose context is her analysis and her father's approaching death. We have reason to wonder what sorts of fantasies occurred to their minds during this analysis. What sort of mourning work did they have to do, these two, analyst and analysand? I suppose that there must have been a work of mourning not only in advance of death but also in the face of its fantasized and unapproachable opposite: Freud's immortalization by his youngest daughter, Anna.

Let me explain. Freud identified death with woman on two occasions: first, in one of his first dreams about the Three Furies; then, in 1913, in an essay that dealt with Shakespeare and the Three Caskets. In a letter to Ferenczi from this period, we learn that the real subject of the latter text was his daughter Anna. Consider the end of this essay, which deals with Shakespeare's *King Lear*, and keep in mind that for Freud the latent subject, Anna, becomes (as in the Irma dream) mother, mother-daughter, and his mother-daughter.

Lear carries Cordelia's dead body on to the stage. Cordelia is Death. If we reverse the situation it becomes intelligible and familiar to us. She is the Death-goddess like the Valkyrie in German mythology who carries away the dead hero from the battlefield. . . . We might argue that what is represented here are the three inevitable relations that a man has with a woman—the woman who bears him, the woman who is his mate and the woman who destroys him; or that they are the three forms taken by the figure of the mother in the course of a man's life—the mother herself, the beloved one who is chosen after her pattern, and lastly the Mother Earth who receives him once more. (*Standard Edition*, 12:301)

The parentheses of the Oedipus complex together encompass inside and outside even unto death. Oddly enough, even though *Three Essays on the Theory of Sexuality* and the book on jokes were written at the same time, there is little erotic material in the latter. This initial split turns out to be on a par with a later split. Freud later emphasizes the son's matricidal desire and the castrating mother's desire for her son. Yet, thanks to the split, it is death, rather than aggression, that is aligned with the mother-daughter. Anna is Thanatos, the signifier that eludes all *analysis* and *anachronism*.

I have already indicated elsewhere (*Freud as a Writer* [1981]) that in *Beyond the Pleasure Principle*, Freud's own description of his grandson's play with the bobbin, as an unconsciously determined mastery with regard to the mother's absence, is itself unconsciously overdetermined. Between the hidden inscription of Freud's name and the manifest presence of his grandson Ernst in *Beyond the Pleasure Principle*, there is the second generation of ana-logy: a past and present Anna, an ana-chronism of differences, an incomparable ana-logy which refers only to itself. Ana, an antithetical preposition which has the sense in Greek of both progression and retrogression, comprises the movement of both drives described in *Beyond the Pleasure Principle* where "beyond" means something more fundamental than the pleasure principle, that is, both beyond and before, an atopical and anachronistic decentering in which everything is deferred. Thus, we are caught in *ana,* whose difference with Anna is an *n,* a letter which is a principal factor in the Irma dream. Nonetheless, its graphic form as chemical symbol and all the rest shows up in neither the manifest nor the latent dream.

Jacques Derrida: *Reply*

I don't know that I would go as far as you have in saying that Freud was so inattentive to play or that he was more concerned with work than with play. There are, clearly, Freudian words and concepts—you read a list of them, but a list is a list—that turn on the notion of work rather than play. Yet one could also find evidence of Freud's interest in play. More than once, he begins a text by talking about child's play. I think that if one becomes fascinated by the classic conceptual opposition of play and work, one may be letting oneself in for an infinite series of combinations. Perhaps it would be better to try to pose the problem differently. I agree with you that, in effect, every time Freud encounters something called play, he is very anxious to *comprehend*—that is, to comprehend the meaning of the play. He does not believe that play is insignificant, that it is purely a game. He believes, then, that there is a limit to play, some operation, some desire, the quest for some gain or profit, et cetera, which is at work in it in whatever way. When there is play—well, it's there and he knows it's there, for the child obviously, but also for the artist. His first concern is to continue the analysis in the face of play. There is another attitude—let us call it obscurantist—that one may adopt toward play which consists in throwing in the towel and saying: "Okay, that's a game. It's gratuitous, play for the sake of play; it means nothing, it's pure expenditure." I would be very wary of this temptation, even though it might fascinate me. I am very wary of it because it would be at this moment that one risks falling short of the scientific, theoretical demand and failing in one's responsibility to try to comprehend what play signifies, what strategies, interests, and investments are at work in play.

In short, what is the economy of play? Freud's interest in it is an economic interest. He tries to see what goes on in play in energetic terms—in terms, that is, of savings and expenditure. I will go even further in Freud's defense and say that he is justified in this by his historical, strategic situation. If right away he had thrown in the towel when faced with play, if he had begun by saying: There is a specificity of play, the specificity of man is play, language is play, period, and that's all—psychoanalysis would have stopped right there. But he had a science to inaugurate, that is to say, an endeavor to find the best account for whatever might appear gratuitous, insignificant, and so forth. I would thus begin by granting for as long as possible Freud's interpretive demand within the field in which he had to struggle to impose an idea of psychoanalysis. When, however—and here I come back toward your position—at a certain moment he had to suppose that there was meaning and finality everywhere, that everything was part of an economy and, consequently, that play was always bordered by something which could be called work, seriousness, the economical, et cetera, here there may in fact be a limit. But the limit is not Freud's. It is the limit of philosophy and science. One could demonstrate that every time a philosophy or a science claims to have constituted its own coherence in some fashion, it has in fact been led to reduce the element of play or to comprehend it by assigning it a place, to hem it in somehow. Well, in this sense, Freud is a classical scholar or philosopher.

In order to make apparent a play that is not comprehended

in this philosophical or scientific space, one must think of play in another way. Indeed, this is what I am trying to do within what is already a tradition—that of Nietzsche, for example—but one which also has its genealogy. On the basis of thinking such as Nietzsche's (as interpreted by [Eugen] Fink), the concept of play, understood as the play *of* the world, is no longer play *in* the world. That is, it is no longer determined and contained by something, by the space that would comprehend it. I believe that it is only on this basis and on this condition that the concept of play can be reconstructed and reconciled with all of the—if you will—"deconstructive"-type notions, such as trace and writing, to which you pointed a moment ago. Once play is no longer simply play in the world, it is also no longer the play of someone who plays. Philosophy has always made play into an activity, the activity of a subject manipulating objects. As soon as one interprets play in the sense of playing, one has already been dragged into the space of classical philosophy where play is dominated by meaning, by its finality, and consequently by something that surpasses and orients it. In order to think of play in a radical way, perhaps one must think beyond the activity of a subject manipulating objects according to or against the rules, et cetera. For a long time now, it is this kind of thinking about play (which is no longer simply playing) that has interested me. This play is not like a game that one plays with, and, naturally, it may be very risky.

In very summary terms, then, this is the principle of what I would have liked to set in motion. The *fort/da** at the center of "Freud's Legacy" is also, of course, a discourse on play. And, typically, Freud indeed does propose an interpretation of the child's game. He piles up hypotheses: the child throws

---

*In *Beyond the Pleasure Principle*, Freud describes a child's play with a bobbin on a string. As he casts it away from him, he utters "o-o-o," which his mother interprets as the word "*fort*" (away, far); as he pulls it back, he says "a-a-a," which according to the mother means "*da*" (here).—Tr.

his bobbin, he brings it back in order to say this or that to his mother, and so forth. I won't attempt to reconstitute here this whole very complicated scene. To be sure, the theme of play is there. However, if one understands the *fort/da* beyond what it seems Freud intends to say, then one may exceed the limits of the game toward the play of the world where the *fort/da* is no longer simply the relation of subject to object. It is, instead, that which has absolute command over all experience in general. To arrive at such a point—and I think I attempt this gesture, in a discreet manner at least, in the course of that text—one must nevertheless begin by reading Freud in a certain way. If one does, then one realizes that basically he does not stop at any single interpretation of the *fort/da*. He evokes several types of interpretations which then generally serve as stopping-points for those who quote and who use Freud. Freud, on the other hand, always ends up finding his interpretations insufficient. One by one, he throws them away and moves on to another. He always has to take one more step: he moves on to another which he also throws away until finally he retains no single interpretation. He himself is doing *fort/da* with his own interpretations, and it never stops. His own writing, his own deportment in this text is doing *fort/da*. Perhaps the performative is in play as well, in a very serious manner, but the game is also very serious and demands great concentration. He plays with this *fort/da* in his writing; he doesn't "comprehend" it. He writes himself this scene, which is descriptive or theoretical but also very profoundly autobiographical and performative to the degree that it concerns him in his relation with his heirs: his grandson, his daughter who, in fact, died a short time after the experience and before he wrote the text. There is, in other words, an immense autobiographical scene invested in this apparently theoretical writing, and it is doing *fort/da*. When this becomes apparent, there is no longer a limit on the *fort/da*. That is, it is no longer a determinate structure, which Freud is interpreting; rather, it is that which has command of his own interpretation, which plays with his text and with his own testament. Such, in any case, is what I have tried to show in that text. In writing _Beyond the Pleasure Principle,_ Freud is writing a textual testament not only as regards his own name and his own family, but as regards the analytic movement which he also constructed in a certain fashion, that is, as a great inheritance, a great institution bearing his name. The history of the analytic situation has to deal with that. It is an institution that can't get along without Freud's name, a practical and theoretical science which for once must come to terms and explain itself with its author's name. Unlike every other science, it cannot set aside or dispense with its founder's name. Mathematics, physics, et cetera, might on occasion celebrate the name of a great physicist or a great mathematician, but the proper name is not a structural part of the corpus of the science or the scientific institution. Psychoanalysis, on the other hand, has been inherited from Freud and accounts for itself with the structure of this inheritance. I think that one must finally decipher his text by means of these questions: the question of inheritance, of the proper name, of the _fort/da,_ of the play of the _fort/da_ infinitely exceeding the limits of the text.

Claude Lévesque: _That Incredible Terrible Thing Which Was Not_

How does one approach—carefully and without deluding oneself too much—the question of autobiography and, in particular, the more obscure, labyrinthine, and perilous question of the autobiography of (giving full play here to the double polarity of that genitive) Jacques Derrida? It is certainly safe to say that confession is not the privileged mode of his writing, and he himself has not failed to remind us that we must always consider the possibility that a confession may be a quotation, a pose, a feint, or a parody. It is nonetheless the case that, for several years now, Derrida seems to be implicating himself more in his writing, or at least more openly. Certain assertions are made in his own name, precisely in the form of confessions. These confessions, as precious and enigmatic as they are rare, discontinuous, and laconic, are delivered with such reticence that, it seems to me (but one may never know), they should be taken for what they appear to be. This one, for example, which continues to haunt me: "Everything I write is terribly autobiographical." Why the "terribly" here, which seems strange, surprising, unusual? In this case, the adverb must be given the meaning that comes directly from its nominative root—"in a manner that inspires terror" (one will have to wonder who or what inspires terror, and in whom)—rather than its more familiar, banalized meaning, as, for example, when one wants to signify the intensity of one's attachment to someone or something. Yet, notice that even the latter sense implies excess and extreme. To say, then, that the totality of what one has written is autobiographical in the extreme, even to excess, means that one has overstepped the mark (of discourse and of knowledge) and reached the perilous threshold. In short, it means that there has been a crossing at the limit, a step beyond to where everything breaks down and is overthrown, where unknowing fascinates knowledge and discourse, luring them outside of the system, outside of language, into a space that we enter only if we no longer are. This is the space of disaster which Blanchot speaks of, the space "which, as the intense, silent, and disastrous affirmation of the outside, undoes solitude and overwhelms thought of any sort" (*Van Velde*, p. 21). It is here that the "terribly" becomes necessary in a certain way, since anyone who would "speak truthfully of himself" cannot avoid being brought to the very edge where he encounters (as he disappears into) the impossible, "a terrible thing," writes Derrida in a text I am going to refer to in a moment. Thus, to tell one's own story is to consort with the terrifying. But this non-science is a gay science, an affirmative knowledge whose origin is its own impossibility. "The proof," writes Blanchot, "that a book of autobiography respects the center of truth around which it is composed may be that such a center draws it toward silence. Whoever sees his book through to the end has not come to the end of himself. If he had, his speech would have been 'cut short.' Yet, the drama—as well as the power—in all 'true' confessions is that one begins to speak only with a view to that moment when one will not be able to continue. There is something to be said which one cannot say: it's not necessarily scandalous, it may be quite banal—a lacuna, a void, an area that shrinks from the light because its nature is the impossibility of being brought to light, a secret without secrecy whose broken seal is muteness itself" (*L'Amitié*, pp. 151–52).

Derrida multiplies the terms—none is privileged—when he tries to name what Nietzsche, [Georges] Bataille, Blanchot, and he himself call the impossible, that which escapes possibility and power, primarily the power of discourse. This unnameable is nevertheless what moves him and drives him, what makes him speak and write: this terrible thing, the incredible thing which is not, this "secret without secrecy" which leads all autobiography toward that point where one can no longer say anything. "I am trying to experience *in my body*," writes Derrida in "Ja, ou le faux-bond," "an altogether other relation to the incredible 'thing which was not.'* It's probably not possible, especially if one wants to make of this experience something other than a consolation, a mourning, a new well-being, a reconcilation with death, although that's not something I sneer at. But this impossibility as regards "the thing that is not" is, finally, the only thing that interests me. It's what I call— awkwardly still—mourning's mourning [*le deuil du deuil*]. It is a *terrible thing* that I do not love but that I want to love. You ask me what makes me write or speak: there it is. It's something like that—not what I love but what I would like to love, what makes me run or wait, bestows and withdraws my idiom. And the re-bon."†

---

*The reference is to the Houyhnhnms' language in *Gulliver's Travels:* "He replied that I must be mistaken, or that I 'said the thing which was not.' (For they have no words in their language to express lying or falsehood.)" Part IV, Chap. III.

†The "good again," or the rebound of the good.—Tr.

For structural reasons, then, as soon as autobiography attempts to see itself through to the end, it is linked to this "terrible thing" which writes and which drives writing, like play come of age that constantly puts everything into play—life, death, speech, writing. It or "she" (autobiography is perhaps inflected in the feminine) pulls on the bobbin's string, bringing it back only in order to send it away, infinitely: *fort/ da*. The idiom—or, if you will, the autobiographical—is always but "the effect of a process of ex-appropriation which produces only perspectives, readings without truth, differences, intersections of affect, a whole 'history' whose very possibility has to be disinscribed and reinscribed." It so happens that the proper name, the patronymic Derrida, inscribes in itself this play of *fort/da* , its process of dispropriation and pluralization. In "Freud's Legacy," Derrida translates *fort* as '*derrière*" (*le rideau* —RIDA), whereas elsewhere, in *Glas*, he openly associates his proper name to the word *derrière* . Thus, "*derrière le rideau*" [behind the curtain] would be the anagram of his name. The German *da* can also be retained, and as a result this double play and double language cut across his name, a foreign name, linguistically heterogeneous, only semi-translated because it cannot be completely translated without loss. In the inscription of his name, Derrida withdraws behind the curtain. He is hidden in the writing, which moves away from itself, does not make its ends meet, repeats, unlimits, and disseminates itself, keeping his name by losing it. "I write in order to lose my name," as Bataille has said.

I have not yet really formulated a question. Here is one: Is there an evolution of Derrida in his relation to Blanchot? I am thinking of a text on [Antonin] Artaud ["La Parole soufflée"], which goes back to 1964, where you say the following: "If clinical commentary and critical commentary everywhere demand their own autonomy and wish to be acknowledged and respected by one another, they are no less complicit . . . in the same abstraction, the same misinterpretation, and the same violence. At the moment when criticism (be it aesthetic, literary, philosophical, et cetera) allegedly protects the meaning of a thought or the value of a work against psychomedical reductions, it comes to the same result [that a reduction would come to] through the opposite path: *it creates an example. That is to say, a case.*" [Michel] Foucault, [Jean] Laplanche, and Blanchot would offer finally but three different ways to neutralize the singularity of a work, thereby missing the graphic in the autobiographic. "Blanchot's meditation stops there: without questioning for themselves either that which irreducibly amounts to Artaud . . . or what is 'untamed' in this experience." Derrida then concludes with an exemplarization, an essentialist reduction of Artaud's discourse. Now, after a fifteen-year interval, when he is trying once again to define the autobiographic, Derrida shows that one cannot avoid this exemplarization with which he seemed to reproach Blanchot. "Autobiography is also the work on the proper name and the signature. This work must be scientific (it must recognize or elaborate laws, that is, utterances with a universal validity) but in a way that each time accounts for singularities that are not simply cases or examples." No more than Blanchot, then, can Derrida avoid the universal law. It is even one of the two simultaneous exigencies irremediably dividing any proper name and all autobiography.

My last question concerns autobiography in its relation to woman. Here I must refer to your development in *Glas* on the transition to ethical self-consciousness in Hegel. It is at the point at which the latter is discussing Sophocles' *Antigone* and the place of femininity in this transition to *Sittlichkeit* [morality] where you write: "Human law, the law of the rational community which is instituted over against the private law of the family, always represses femininity, rises up against her, binds her, presses in upon her, and restrains her. But masculine potency has a limit—an essential and eternal one: the weapon, doubtless an impotent one, the all-powerful weapon of the impotent, the inalienable stroke of woman is irony. Woman, 'internal enemy of the community,' can always burst out laughing at the last moment. She knows, in sorrow and in death, how to pervert the power that represses her."

My question is this: If, on the one hand, man's substantial, effective life is in the State, in science but also in war and in work—that is, grappling with the vast external world—and, on the other hand, if woman, with her irony, her veils, and her lies, is allied with the singularity of the unconscious, then can one say that autobiography—if it would see itself through to the end—can be produced only as the autobiography of the woman, in both senses of that genitive? In autobiography, only femininity would lend itself to understanding, only femininity would lead one to hear and understand the singular secret that constitutes it. Only a feminine writing—in the sense in which you speak of it in *Spurs*—can (even as it cannot) tell its story as the unrelenting quest of that terrible thing which opens language to its own beyond.

Jacques Derrida: *Reply*

I am going to try to answer. Although I would like to avoid giving in to an auto-explanation which can very quickly turn into an auto-justification, even auto-celebration, the situation requires somewhat that I do so. Having said that, I am going to try to remain very neutral. Obviously, I agree entirely with what you said at the beginning about the disseminated name "*derrière le rideau*," which, already in *Glas*, was the object of a certain amount of work. And you're right, playing with one's own name, putting it in play, is, in effect, what is always going on and what I have tried to do in a somewhat more explicit or systematic manner for some time now and in certain texts. But obviously this is not something one can decide: one doesn't disseminate or play with one's name. The very structure of the proper name sets this process in motion. That's what the proper name is for. At work, naturally, in the desire—the apparent desire—to lose one's name by disarticulating it, disseminating it, is the inverse movement. By disseminating or losing my own name, I make it more and more intrusive; I occupy the whole site, and as a result my name gains more ground. The more I lose, the more I gain by conceiving my proper name as the common noun "*derrière le rideau*," and so on. The more, also, I monumentalize my proper name. So now every time you utter the word "*derrière*," you'll be paying a tax to my name, settling up what you owe. The dissemination of a proper name is, in fact, a way of seizing the language, putting it to one's own use, instating its law. Tomorrow, perhaps, during the discussion of translation, we will come back to this in talking about the story of Babel, because that is what Babel is: the story of God's proper name. To lose one's name by transforming it into a common name or pieces of a common name is also to celebrate it. One takes the risk of losing one's name by winning it, and vice versa. This always happens as soon as there is some proper name: the scene is in place where one loses what one wins and wins what one loses. It is one of the scenes of the *double bind* in *Glas*, and what I there tried to organize around the proper name—not only mine, of course, because I was also concerned with other proper names which are subjected to the same operation, which is naturally different and singular every time. The operation comes into play differently with the names of [Francis] Ponge, Hegel, Blanchot, et cetera.

Thus, the proper name is at play and it's meant to play all by itself, to win or lose the match without me. This is to say that, at the furthest limit, I no longer need to pull the strings myself, to write one way or another. It is written like that by itself. When it comes to names, the relation between the proper and the common already programs the whole scenario.

In order not to keep the floor too long, I'll get on to your next question on the subject of Blanchot. There has doubtless been on my part a certain distance traveled in relation to Blanchot. However, I would not understand it only with regard to the problem of exemplarity, unicity, and so forth. The evolution is so—what shall I say?—so obvious that there's no need to wait ten or fifteen years. It is said in the same text, at the end. One must take into account the rhetoric of that text on Artaud, as well as its own logic and the play that is being played out there. At the end of the text, I put in question once again the apparent accusation I launch against Blanchot by saying that I myself have given in to the same operation—in other words, that I have in turn fashioned an example and that this gesture is inevitable. There is a rotation at the end of "La Parole soufflée" which shows that I have done and that I had to do exactly what, at the beginning, I seemed to reproach Blanchot, Foucault, and Laplanche for doing, which is to say that I have once again made an example and that this gesture is irreducible. Thus, in a certain way, this is not an evolution: the move is immediate.

On the other hand and from another point of view, it is true that the work of Blanchot has been very decisive for me. At first, by attaching myself especially to Blanchot's so-called critical or theoretical text, I thought I had introjected, interiorized, assimilated Blanchot's contribution and had brought it to bear in my work, although obviously in another language. In a certain way, I thought I had read Blanchot. And then, rather recently, a few years ago, I read what I had never managed to read in a way which was at bottom—how shall I say?—an experience. I began to read or to reread certain of Blanchot's *récits* and to discover certain of those texts that I thought I had read but which I had not really succeeded in reading before. I must say that in relation to Blanchot's narrative or fictional texts (actually these words are insufficient and I don't know what to call them), there then seemed to me to be a space opening up which was far less easy to dominate and to assimilate than a certain type of Blanchot's discursiveness that I thought I could assimilate from the so-called theoretical/critical texts. In relation to these former texts, the work to be done seems to me infinite. From this point of view, then, my relation to Blanchot's text has been transformed and I feel far more overwhelmed by that text than I thought I was at a given moment, for example at the time of "La Parole soufflée." This overwhelming is of another sort than the one I have already mentioned.

Now, as for femininity: Here too, at the risk of being very succinct, I will be brief. What you alluded to was not exactly part of that text on Nietzsche (*Spurs*) but was the answer to a question during the debate that followed. I asked of my questioner: "Are you asking me an autobiographical question? Well, yes, I would like to write, which is not to say that I will write, but that I would like to write in a woman's hand"—or something like that.

Having cleared up this point, and in order to get back right away to the formulation which you justified by an earlier development, I subscribe with little difficulty to the formula "autobiography of the woman." However, this formula becomes very indeterminate and the way the "of" may come into play is what's interesting. The autobiography of the woman: that means that my autobiography, for example, the autobiography of someone whose writing, apparently, is masculine, is the autobiography *of* a woman, as in an emanation *of*, which is to say that my autobiography signs itself (and there is a play of pronouns here) beginning precisely with the addressee who signs. It is the addressee who signs. So, if I want to tell the story of my life, it is an addressee, an "I" marked in the feminine, who will sign and who will therefore be—I won't say the author because that word immediately destroys everything—but the place from which something like my biography, my autobiography will be signed. In other words, it will not be an autobiography, naturally, but a heterobiography in the sense in which one also says heterosexuality, and so on. Thus, it will be the autobiography of the woman, hers, or of her(s), from her, descending from her, as if inherited if from her, from a woman, of the woman. All this does not mean that she can be identified, that there is only one of her. Rather, each time it is she, it is you who signs the text by receiving it. When I say "by receiving it," when I make use of that used-up language of communication (emission, reception, address, addresser, addressee), I may seem to imply that it's man who writes and woman—some woman, a woman addressee—who signs and who is first of all herself an addressee. Here, then, one would have to make a correction. Let us say that autobiography is not necessarily the man who writes and the woman who receives, sealing and arresting the signature and the message by her reception. Instead, let us say that she already writes when I write. What in the old terminology is called the addressee is here already in the process of writing in my place, and this implies all the possibilities of combination that such a "lending each other a hand" might have in a situation like that.

Eugene Vance: *The Ear of the Heart*

In "Freud's Legacy" and here in "Otobiographies," you have analyzed two thinkers who are singular in that they are, in their proper names, entirely, personally engaged in their texts, with all the risks you say that involves. I myself think that we have an undeniable interest in analyzing as well certain autobiographical projects from a far more distant past. In particular, I am thinking of autobiographies whose signatories refer explicitly to a transcendent and infinite being, and who thus enlist this infinite being in their own accounts of themselves. Thus, I would like to say a few words about Saint Augustine's *Confessions.* I want to talk about a problematic of the knowledge of truth in relation to the desire of the writing subject for a return to an origin without alterity.

First, a word about Saint Augustine's trinitarian theology. There is first the originating Father who gives himself to the created world, or who bestows creation in the person of his Son. By his acts and words among men, this Son inspired a biographical text—the Gospels—whose profound truth belongs not only to the Son but also to the Father who is the author and signatory of the world. Man's cognition of this Father begins with a (re)cognition of the Son, but it is only through the Holy Spirit that man arrives at an immaterial knowledge of God. It is through this same "ear of the heart," the Holy Spirit, that man accedes to the kernel of hidden truth beneath the shell of the evangelical text.

On an epistemological level, the knowledge of truth is produced in the soul in several distinct stages. First, we experience an illumination, a flash of light which inundates us. This flash, however, is not at all lasting; it is already hidden at the very moment it presents itself to the mind. Yet it leaves traces (*vestigia*) or impressions (*impressiones*) in our memories which constitute a kind of prelinguistic and purely mental writing. This writing is not produced by God himself, however, but by and in the mind of the subject visited by the illumination. There is thus a difference between the flash of light and the impressions produced in the memory, but it's a minor difference. As part of the soul, memory is of a spiritual rather than a material nature, and therefore the text produced there is adequate to the illumination it represents. However, we retain these traces in our memory for only a brief moment, during which we assign verbal signifiers to them, whether or not these signifiers are vocalized. Here, then, is a second difference: The *signans* is outside the *signatum*, and signifies it only by convention rather than by nature. But signs uttered by the voice are themselves also ephemeral, so that in order to fix them in time and in space, man invented written signs, letters. These written signs are maximally different from the original truth they are summoned to represent.

This, then, is a diagram of epistemic differentiation on several levels which serves as the matrix for Saint Augustine's autobiographical project. That account begins with Saint Augustine's earliest childhood. At this stage, *logos* is given to the baby not as an instantaneous flash but as mother's milk. It is the pure gift of life, a life that as yet has neither inside nor outside. Alienation begins very slowly for the baby; smiles preferred during sleep are the index of a nascent independent will. Then the child devotes himself to the acquisition of human language, during which time he moves from the mastery of natural signs to that of conventional signs. This is Saint Augustine's first fall into the abyss, into the "region of difference" (*regio dissimilitudinis*). Saint Augustine's formal education begins with an initiation into the *grammatica*, the science both of written signs and of the grammatical laws that are the foundation of language. But the Latin language and the corpus which were the object of the *grammatica* were surely altogether other for him, since we may be quite sure that this boy from the North African plains spoke a patois and not the classical Latin he studied. Next, he learned Greek, a totally alien language whose apprenticeship was odious to him. Who dispensed this instruction? It was a grammarian whose pedagogy, like a horse-trainer's, relied on the whip. The whip is the institutional legacy of the sin of Adam—the father of us all—and its justice is dispensed according to the ancient Law of a Father who is very angry at the sons of Adam. Thus, for Augustine the liberal arts are a form of slavery, a spiritual labor to which man was condemned following his sin and his exile from paradise. From *grammatica*, the child moves on to rhetoric, the most vain of all the sciences of discourse (*artes sermocinales*). Learning rhetoric had the effect of alienating Augustine from the Gospels, whose discourse seemed to him unworthy of Cicero's. Spiritual exile from original truth was now accomplished, rather, *nearly* acomplished, since his mother was a Christian and was praying continually for his conversion.

This estrangement from the ultimate meaning of everything, this exile in the external shell of language, prepares, however, the conclusion of Augustine's autobiography. That autobiography does not take the discursive form of a closed *récit*; rather, it takes that of a return to the Father in the form of an exegesis of the biblical text. Thus, having been reborn to life through Christ and illuminated by the Holy Spirit, Augustine joyfully closes his *Confessions* with a long explication of the first verses of Genesis which tell the story of God's creation of the universe. His abandonment of the narrative of his personal origins in favor of an exegesis of the creation story is a "literary" strategy that imposes precise limits on the autobiographical enterprise, even on the institution of literature itself.

I hope that one may recognize in my improvised remarks certain themes that Jacques Derrida has evoked in "Otobiographies." In both cases, it is a question of credit, of credibility. Saint Augustine says that one must read his autobiographical text charitably, with credit—the reader must give him credit. As for Augustine himself, his interlocutor is God. Thus God gives himself credit by allowing Augustine to compose his text, which God knows already because God knows everything. Here is an attempt to inculcate, to establish a metaphysic in an otherwise different—and deficient—discourse of selfhood.

I would like to conclude by suggesting that it is probably just as difficult for someone to *construct* an autobiographical text that opens fully onto the metaphysical as it is for us to *deconstruct* an autobiographical text in which the metaphysical is repressed. One of modernity's distortions, perhaps, is to tend to make us disregard any effort toward a positive construction no matter how much lucidity it displays. One should take these remarks as a plea for history, though not at all as a defense of the game of the talented precursor. On the contrary, my remarks are an invitation to read those texts which constitute another side of modernity and which give it—or deprive it of—another meaning.

Jacques Derrida: *Reply*

I don't know what authorizes me more than someone else to take the floor again here. I listened with great interest to this rich and fascinating analysis. One is struck by a certain number of startling analogies. How far does the analogy work? What will prove to be its significance? What will establish the criteria for making distinctions? It's rather difficult to say. Although answers might come quickly, they are surely naive. Thus, for example, one could say: In the case of Augustine, it is finally God who is presumed to sign within the same structure; but God and the eternal return are not the same thing. That's a little facile, I admit, and one can't stop there. One must try to go further, because it may be that God and the eternal return—when both are thought without facileness—are not as opposed as they might appear to be. But I would not want to force this argument too far. There is another question, however, concerning the possible generality of an autobiographical structure. It may be that the same program and basically the same scene recurs regularly. Within this scene or this relational system, the terms might change. The Judeo-Christian name might be replaced by another name, which would, however, have the same function. Each moment or each instance may be variable in its content, but the law of the relation between the variables would remain the same. Each time one had an autobiographical scene to stage, one would come upon the same structure again, so that Saint Augustine, Nietzsche, and a few others—Rousseau, perhaps, or Montaigne—could only come along and fill in a trellis or a grid which is already in place and which in some way would not in itself be historical.

Eugene Vance

Can modernity escape that determinism?

Jacques Derrida: *Reply*

No, no. As for me, I'm no fan of modernity. I have no simple belief in the irreducible specificity of "modernity." I even wonder if I have ever used that word. In any case, I am very mistrustful whenever people identify historical breaks or when they say, "This begins there." I have never done that, and I believe I have even set down here and there reservations with regard to this type of periodization and distribution. That's why I am very interested in work of this type, even though my training, my lack of knowledge places many limits on me. I'm convinced that one could expand this kind of research. It's not a question of precursors—the notion of a precursor here would efface all the originality of the thing— but of recurrences which would not efface the singularity or the idiom of each text. Whatever one might say about the resemblance between the Nietzschean autobiography and the Augustinian autobiography, it's really another language in every sense of the word. However, nothing of the signature's idiom is lost when one points to the recurrence, the regularity with which the scene returns. This is precisely the paradox of the proper name or the signature: It's always the same thing, but each time it's different; each time it's a different history to which one must pay close attention. In this way one may see that, in spite of everything, finally—and this is where I began—Nietzsche attempted something which, in relation to the Christian unfolding of this scene, was, precisely, of a "deconstructive" type.

Now, you asked a question about deconstruction which I am trying to reconstitute and you will tell me if I do so inaccurately. You wondered whether, instead of deconstructing, it would not be interesting to attempt, well, a more positive gesture, perhaps an autobiographically deconstructive writing . . .

Eugene Vance

No. I would say that it seems to me just as interesting to study constructions that don't work as it is to practice deconstructions that don't work either, that is, which don't entirely succeed.

Jacques Derrida: _Reply_

Yes, I agree. But here you are referring to a diagram of deconstruction which would be that of a technical operation used to dismantle systems. Personally, I don't subscribe to this model of deconstruction. What was said earlier, particularly by Claude Lévesque, demonstrates that what has been called the deconstructive gesture (in a moment I will try to say a little more about this) is accompanied, or can be accompanied (in any case, I would hope to accompany it), by an affirmation. It is not negative, it is not destructive. This is why the word "deconstruction" has always bothered me. Yesterday, during a session at McGill University, someone asked me a question about the word "deconstruction." I said that when I made use of this word (rarely, very rarely in the beginning—once or twice—so you can see that the paradox of the message transformed by the addressees is fully in play here), I had the impression that it was a word among many others, a secondary word in the text which would fade or which in any case would assume a non-dominant place in a system. For me, it was a word in a chain with many other words—such as trace or differance*—as well as with a whole elaboration which is not limited only to a lexicon, if you will. It so happens—and this is worth analyzing—that this word which I had written only once or twice (I don't even remember where exactly) all of a sudden jumped out of the text and was seized by others who have since determined its fate in the manner you well know. Faced with this, I myself then had to justify myself, to explain, to try to get some leverage. But precisely because of the technical and—how shall I put it?—negative connotations that it could have in certain contexts, the word by itself bothered me. I do think it is also necessary to dismantle systems, to analyze structures in order to see what's going on, both when things work and when they don't, why structures don't manage to close themselves off, and so forth. But for me "deconstruction" was not at all the first or the last word, and certainly not a password or slogan for everything that was to follow.

Claude Lévesque

Doesn't the word come from Heidegger?

Jacques Derrida: *Reply*

Yes. When I made use of this word, I had the sense of translating two words from Heidegger at a point where I needed them in the context. These two words are *Destruktion*, which Heidegger uses, explaining that *Destruktion* is not a destruction but precisely a destructuring that dismantles the structural layers in the system, and so on. The other word is *Abbau*, which has a similar meaning: to take apart an edifice

*See above, p. xii.

in order to see how it is constituted or deconstituted. This is classic. What was not so classic, however, was what this force, this _Abbau_, was applied to: the whole of classical ontology, the whole history of Western philosophy. The word got highlighted in the context of the period, which was more or less dominated by structuralism. The watchword being "structure, structure, structure," when someone says destructure, destructuring, or deconstruction, well, then it acquires a pertinence which personally I didn't pay too much attention to. To be sure, I wasn't altogether inattentive to this word either, but also I was not—how shall I say?—involved; I had not organized things to such an extent around this word. When others got involved in it, I tried to determine this concept in my own manner, that is, according to what I thought was the right manner, which I did by insisting on the fact that it was not a question of a negative operation. I don't feel that I'm in a position to _choose_ between an operation that we'll call negative or nihilist, an operation that would set about furiously dismantling systems, and the other operation. I love very much everything that I deconstruct in my own manner; the texts I want to read from the deconstructive point of view are texts I love, with that impulse of identification which is indispensable for reading. They are texts whose future, I think, will not be exhausted for a long time. For example, I think Plato is to be read, and read constantly. Plato's signature is not yet finished—that's the destiny of signatures—nor is Nietzsche's, nor is Saint Augustine's (like you, I'm altogether convinced of that), nor are the signatures of still many others. Thus, if my relation to these texts is characterized by loving jealousy and not at all by nihilistic fury (one can't read anything in the latter condition), then I don't feel I'm in a position to choose according to the terms in which you have presented the choice.

Pierre Jacques: _Question from the Floor_

You have talked about the anterior addressee, which is to say the dead, as well as about the future addressee. But what happens to the fulfillment and the genre of the signature when the addresser is the addressee? What happens when Nietzsche writes, finally, to himself?

Jacques Derrida: *Reply*

What happens? But when you say he writes himself, you seem to assume that he already has his identity, that he is already himself.

Pierre Jacques

No, I don't assume it. That's what I'm asking.

Jacques Derrida: *Reply*

No, he is not yet himself when he is in the situation, precisely, of distance from the other, the other's distance. When he writes himself to himself, he *writes himself to the other* who is infinitely far away and who is supposed to send his signature back to him. He has no relation to himself that is not forced to defer itself by passing through the other in the form, precisely, of the eternal return. I love what I am living and I desire what is coming. I recognize it gratefully and I desire it to return eternally. I desire whatever comes my way to come to me, and to come back to me eternally. When he writes himself to himself, he has no immediate presence of himself to himself. There is the necessity of this detour through the other in the form of the eternal return of that which is affirmed, of the wedding and the wedding ring, of the alliance. The motif of the alliance or wedding ring, of the hymen or marriage, returns often in Nietzsche, and this "yes, yes" has to be thought beginning with the eternal return. I want it to return by making the round which is the cycle of the sun or the annual cycle, of the annulus, of the year which annuls itself by coming back around on itself. This is why so much importance is given to the anniversary and to the midday sun's return upon itself. From this point of view, there is no differ-

ence, or no possible distinction if you will, between the letter
I write to someone else and the letter I send to myself. The
structure is the same. Within this common structure, there
would, of course, be a difference. If I write myself a letter,
address it to myself at my address, go put it in the mailbox,
then wait for it to come back to me—and plenty of accidents
can occur in the meantime—that's not exactly the same thing
as when I send a letter to someone else in the everyday sense
of the term. But this is a subdifference. The fundamental
structure of the dispatch is the same.

ROUNDTABLE ON TRANSLATION

Translated by Peggy Kamuf

Claude Lévesque: *Introduction*

There are obvious links between autobiography, the subject of yesterday's discussion, and translation, our question for to-day. Autobiography—the autobiographical genre—has some-thing to do with genealogy and with the proper name. This work on the proper name, on all that is invested in it, repre-sents an attempt to inscribe the unique in the system of lan-guage, and the narrative account in the concept. The point is that translation cannot help meeting on its way the problem of the proper name and the question of idiomatic language within the body of writing. When Derrida tells us what he understands and intends by the proper name, he almost al-ways appeals to the motif of translation and most particularly to that which resists any transposition from one language to another. In "Freud's Legacy," he writes: "Any signified whose signifier cannot vary nor let itself be translated into another signifier without a loss of meaning points to a proper-name effect." In fact, there are two simultaneous demands governing the proper name which one must not be too quick to separate from each other: on the one hand, a requirement of untranslat-ability and unreadability, as if the proper name were nothing but pure reference, lying outside of signification and language; on the other hand, a requirement of translatability and read-ability, as if the proper name were assimilable to the common noun, to any word that is caught up in a linguistic and genea-logical network where meaning already contaminates non-meaning and where the proper name is absorbed and expro-priated by the common noun.

On the political level, this undecidable double postulation of the particular and the universal is translated in the form of a contradictory opposition between, for example, nationalism and universalism. Derrida writes in "Living On: Borderlines": "What this institution [the university] cannot bear is for any-one to tamper with language, meaning both the national language and, paradoxically, an ideal of translatability that neu-tralizes this national language. *Nationalism and universalism.* What this institution cannot bear is a transformation that leaves intact neither of these two complementary poles."

But now let us ask ourselves what has been happening here since yesterday in this double session which reduplicates aca-demic discourse (scientific as well as philosophical) with a whole dimension which that discourse can only reject because it undermines the ideal of total translatability, the very basis of the idea of a university. If it is true that the philosopher and the scholar share an ideal of universality which abstracts the proper name, the biographical, as well as the corruptions of nationalism and of dialect, then it may begin to appear that around the table here today there are neither scholars nor philosophers nor academics. It may appear that an undermin-ing operation is in process which is perhaps no more than the parody of the scholar, the philosopher, and the academic.

Patrick Mahony: *Transformations and Patricidal Deconstruction*

Hearing the word "translation," one thinks immediately of its etymological and semantic connections with metaphor, transfer, transference, and transport. And, of course, the apho-rism "*traduttore, traditore*"* may come to mind simultane-ously. In this regard, and since my approach is of a psycho-analytic nature, I cannot resist beginning with a somewhat humorous aside which unites the notions of treason and trans-port. Given that the diagnosis of schizophrenia is much more frequent in America than it is in Europe, if ever someone were to be diagnosed here as schizophrenic, then the cheapest cure would be quite simply for him to book passage on a transat-lantic ship. It's a case of translation curing translation. But now, let's be serious.

In an essay which attempted to give a global classification of

---

*"Translator, traitor."—Tr.

translation's linguistic aspects, [Roman] Jakobson distinguished three kinds of translation:

1 intralingual translation, or paraphrase;

2 interlingual translation, or translation in the most common sense;

3 intersemiotic translation, in which, for example, verbal signs are reencoded in nonverbal sign systems.

The conservatism of Jakobson's approach contrasts with the audacity of your own procedure, which one of your commentators, Sarah Kofman, has summarized as follows: "Derrida's originality is to put an end to a process of translation and decision by a formal, syntactic practice of undecidability" (*Ecarts*, p. 182).

The first question I will ask refers to the use of the specific term "translation" instead of "transformation," which would describe your procedure in a much more adequate fashion. I am referring to three of your writings: "Freud and the Scene of Writing" (1967); your interview in *Positions* (1972); as well as your introduction, "Me—Psychoanalysis," to Nicolas Abraham's "The Shell and the Kernel" (1979). In the first text, you show that certain of Freud's uses of the term "translation" are really transformations and/or metaphorical uses. Then, in "Me—Psychoanalysis," you comment on Abraham's theories as follows: " 'Translation' preserves a symbolic and anasemic relation to translation, to what one calls 'translation.' " In fact, in *Positions*, you propose the term "transformation" as a far more adequate notion. Thus you say: "In the limits to which it is possible or at least *appears* possible, translation practices the difference between signified and signifier. But if this difference is never pure, no more so is translation, and for the notion of translation we would have to substitute a notion of *transformation*: a regulated transformation of one language by another, of one text by another."

It seems to me, moreover, that *transformation* is more in harmony with your neologism *tranche-fert*,* the key concept of

*See Derrida's remarks, pp. 104–05, below, for an explanation of this neologism.—Tr.

your essay "Du tout" ["Of the Whole"] which justly contests the limits of psychoanalytic transference. Let us recall that early on Freud conceived the latter as a set of "false connections" and considered every isolated act and each of the analysand's associations as a compromise (*Standard Edition*, 12:103). Since, moreover, all of the patient's utterances are more or less closely tied to the *tranche-fert* or the false connection, could we not conceive psychoanalysis as a semiotic of approximations, or, better still, a semiotic of decentered transformations? Indeed, in *Fors*, you show, on the one hand, that these transformations are operating according to a radical and interminable deviation (here one thinks of the possible cleavage of the crypt in the id and the ego) and, on the other, that a written case is but an asymptotic place of "convergences" for all the possible translations and betrayals, an interminable approximation of the idiom.

In order to think about these decentered transformations somewhat differently, one could take as a guide and by way of a specific example the following consideration: Throughout our lives, we acquire a series of names, beginning with the nicknames and names of endearment from childhood all the way to the formal titles and other names of adulthood. One of the characteristics of clinical discourse in the analytic context, which sets it apart from all other formal or intimate discourses, is that one almost never addresses the patient by any of these names which are so egocentrically bound up with him. By setting off the discharge of forgotten material to fill the void, this narcissistic deprivation also induces the patient to let himself go toward multiple transpositions and transformations of his names, whose many vicissitudes can be approached only by further research.

On a strictly terminological plane, I have done a thorough inventory of the word "translation"—*Übersetzung*—in all of Freud's texts. While he considers repression to be a rift or fault in the translation, on several occasions in his writings he implicitly conceives all of the following to be translations: hysterical, phobic, and obsessional symptoms, dreams, recollections, parapraxes, the choice of the means of suicide, the choice of fetish, the analyst's interpretations, and the transpositions of unconscious material to consciousness. However, while on occasion Freud specifically uses the word "translation" as a synonym for "transformation," this latter term seems to be used only with reference to the process of libidinal development, as one may easily discern from titles such as "On Transformations of Instinct as Exemplified in Anal Erotism" or "The Transformations of Puberty" (Part 3 of _Three Essays on the Theory of Sexuality_). But it is in the context of your very provocative and stimulating reflections on sexuality that I would like to interrogate the notion of transformation and the meaning you give it.

1. In your introduction to Abraham's "The Shell and the Kernel," you write: "In 1968 the anasemic interpretation certainly bore primarily on Freudian and post-Freudian problematics: metapsychology, Freud's 'pansexualism' which was the 'anasemic (pansexualism) of the Kernel,' that 'nucleic sex' which was supposed to have 'no relation with the difference between sexes' and about which Freud is supposed to have said, 'again anasemically, that it is in essence virile' (that it seems to me is one of the most enigmatic and provocative passages in the essay)."

2. In _Spurs: Nietzsche's Styles,_ you have written: "There is no essence of the woman because woman separates and separates from herself."

3. In the same essay in _Ecarts,_ Sarah Kofman notes: "The voice of truth is always that of the law, of God, of the father. The metaphysical logos has an essential virility. Writing, that form of disruption of presence, is, like the woman, always put down and reduced to the lowest rung. Like the feminine genitalia, it is troubling, petrifying—it has a Medusa effect" (pp. 125–26). And again: "Perhaps, as well, it is in reading Derrida that one best understands certain psychoanalytic motifs. Derridean writing relentlessly repeats the murder of the father. The many decapitations of the logos in all its forms have to have an effect on the unconscious scene of each reader. More

than Freud, Derrida makes one know what a father means, that one is never through 'killing' the father, and that to speak of the logos as a father is not a simple metaphor" (p. 202).

The passages I have just quoted call up two additional remarks:

1. I would like you to comment further on sexual differentiation.

2. There are those who openly admit to you their inability to imitate your style. It seems to me that the implications of this are far-reaching. Whatever the filiation of your writing may be, with its inimitable trait of the murder of the paternal *logos*, it is nonetheless the case that, on another level, it bears the imprint of the father's attributes.

Such a situation leads us to the consideration that writing is a constantly transformed and transforming activity.

Jacques Derrida: *Reply**

I am going to begin by taking two examples. *Finnegans Wake* is for us today the major corpus, the great challenge to translation, although certainly not the only one. However, a Babelian motif runs from one end of *Finnegans Wake* to the other. Although this motif takes many different forms, which I can't go into now, at a certain moment, referring to the event of the Tower of Babel, at the moment when Yahweh interrupts the construction of the tower and condemns humanity to the multiplicity of languages—which is to say, to the necessary and impossible task of translation—Joyce writes (and here I isolate these three words only for the convenience of our discussion, even though it would be necessary to reconstitute the whole page, all the pages): "And he war." That's what one reads at a certain moment on one page of *Finnegans Wake* in an episode concerning Babel. In what language is this written? Obviously, despite the multiplicity of languages, cultural ref-

---

*Unfortunately, the beginning of Jacques Derrida's reply to Patrick Mahony was not recorded.

erences, and condensations, English is indisputably the dominant language in *Finnegans Wake*—all of these refractions and
slippages are produced in English or through English, in the
body of that language. French would translate the English as:
il-guerre [he wars], he declares war. And that's indeed what
happens: God declares war on the tribe of the Shems, who
want to make a name for themselves by raising the tower and
imposing their tongue on the universe. But obviously the German word *war* influences the English word, so we also have:
He was, he was the one who said, for example, "I am that I
am," which is the definition of Yahweh. And then one also
hears the ear, which is very present in the rest of the text. One
hears a thousand things through other tongues.

I don't want to explore all the possibilities that are con-
densed in these questions, but I wonder what happens at the
moment one tries to translate these words. Even if by some
miracle one could translate all of the virtual impulses at work
in this utterance, one thing remains that could never be translated: the fact that there are two tongues here, or at least more
than one. By translating everything into French, at best one
would translate all of the virtual or actual content, but one
could not translate the event which consists in grafting several
tongues onto a single body.

I will take another example: [Jorge Luis] Borges' "Pierre
Ménard." This text gives the account of a Frenchman who has
conceived the mad project of writing, for the first time, *Don
Quixote*. That's all there is to it: He wants to write not a version,
not a repetition or a parody, but *Don Quixote* itself. This project
comes out of a mad, absolutely raving jealousy. Borges' text is
written in Spanish, but it is marked by the French atmosphere.
Pierre Ménard is a Frenchman, the story takes place in Nîmes,
and there are all sorts of resonances that led Borges to write this
text in a Spanish tongue which is very subtly marked by a
certain Frenchness. Once, in a seminar on translation, I had a
discussion with a Hispanist student who said about this text:
"In the end, the French translation is perhaps more faithful and
thus better than the original." Well, yes and no, because what is
lost in the French translation is this superimposed Frenchness

or the Frenchness that inserts a slight division within the Spanish, all of which Borges wanted to mark in the original. Translation can do everything except mark this linguistic difference inscribed in the language, this difference of language systems inscribed in a single tongue. At best, it can get everything across except this: the fact that there are, in one linguistic system, perhaps several languages or tongues. Sometimes—I would even say always—several tongues. There is impurity in every language. This fact would in some way have to threaten every linguistic system's integrity, which is presumed by each of Jakobson's concepts. Each of these three concepts (intralingual translation, interlingual or translation "properly speaking," and intersemiotic translation) presumes the existence of one language and of one translation in the literal sense, that is, as the passage from one language into another. So, if the unity of the linguistic system is not a sure thing, all of this conceptualization around translation (in the so-called proper sense of translation) is threatened.

I chose the example of Babel because I think it can provide an epigraph for all discussions of translation. What happens in the story of Babel? We think we know that story, but it is always in our interest, I believe, to reread it closely. Also, one should read it if possible in the language in which it was written, because the singularity of the story is that a performative takes place as a *récit* in a tongue that itself defies translation. What is being told in this biblical *récit* is not transportable into another tongue without an essential loss. I don't know the original language thoroughly, but I know enough of it (a few words) to try to define with you this challenge to translation.

What happens in the Babel episode, in the tribe of the Shems? Notice that the word "shem" already means *name*: Shem equals name. The Shems decide to raise a tower—not just in order to reach all the way to the heavens but also, it says in the text, to make a name for themselves. They want to make a name for themselves, and they bear the name of name. So they want to make a name for themselves—how will they do it? By imposing their tongue on the entire universe on the basis of this sublime edification. Tongue: actually the Hebrew word here is the word that signifies lip. Not tongue but lip. Thus, they want to impose their lip on the entire universe. Had their enterprise succeeded, the universal tongue would have been a particular language imposed by violence, by force, by violent hegemony over the rest of the world. It would not have been a universal language—for example in the Leibnizian sense—a transparent language to which everyone would have had access. Rather, the master with the most force would have imposed this language on the world and, by virtue of this fact, it would have become the universal tongue. This, then, is their project: to make a name for themselves by imposing their lip on the world. God—that God who is capable of resentment, jealousy, and anger—becomes beside himself in the face of this incredible effrontery and says to himself: So that's what they want to do, they want to make a name for themselves and impose their lip on the world. He then interrupts the edification and in turn imposes his name on their tower (or his tower). The text says: God proclaimed his name loudly, the name which he himself has chosen and which is thus his. Already one can see that the conflict is a war between two proper names and the one that will carry the day is the one that either imposes its law or in any case prevents the other from imposing its own. God says: Babel. It is thus a proper name. Voltaire, in the article "Babel" in the *Diction-naire philosophique*, says something like this: "It seems that Babel means the name of the father in this case, as in Babylon, et cetera, so it can be translated as the name of the father's city." But all the same, Babel can be understood within the language of the *récit* and only within that language. It can be understood confusedly because it is by virtue of a somewhat free phonetic association that this confusion is possible. It can be confusedly understood as "confusion"—it is a word that will come to signify confusion. He imposes confusion on them at the same time as he imposes his proper name, the name he has chosen which means confusion, which seems confusedly to mean confusion and which the Shems understand in their tongue, confusedly, as confusion. Here, one might conclude that the translation is intralingual, but that would be incorrect since it is a question of a proper name. To translate Babel by "confusion" is already to give a confused and uncertain translation. It translates a proper name into a common noun. Thus one sees that God declares war by forcing men, if you will, to translate his proper name with a common noun. In effect, he says to them: Now you will not impose a single tongue; you will be condemned to the multipliciy of tongues; translate and, to begin with, translate my name. Translate my name, says he, but at the same time he says: You will not be able to translate my name because, first of all, it's a proper name and, secondly, my name, the one I myself have chosen for this tower, signifies ambiguity, confusion, et cetera. Thus God, in his rivalry with the tribe of the Shems, gives them, in a certain way, an absolutely double command. He imposes a double bind on them when he says: Translate me and what is more don't translate me. I desire that you translate me, that you translate the name I impose on you; and at the same time, whatever you do, don't translate it, you will not be able to translate it.

I would say that this desire is at work in every proper name: translate me, don't translate me. On the one hand, don't translate me, that is, respect me as a proper name, respect my law of the proper name which stands over and above all languages. And, on the other hand, translate me, that is, understand me, preserve me within the universal language, follow my law, and so on. This means that the division of the proper name, insofar as it is the division of God—in a word, insofar as it divides God himself—in some way provides the paradigm for this work of the proper name. God himself is in the double bind, God as the deconstructor of the Tower of Babel. He interrupts a construction. The deconstruction of the Tower of Babel, moreover, gives a good idea of what deconstruction is: an unfinished edifice whose half-completed structures are visible, letting one guess at the scaffolding behind them. He interrupts the construction in his name; he interrupts himself in order to impose his name and thus produces what one could call a "disschemination"* which means: You will not impose your meaning or your tongue, and I, God, therefore oblige you to submit to the plurality of languages which you will never get out of.

Yet the original text was absolutely original; it is the sacred text. As [Walter] Benjamin says, the model of all translation is the intralinear translation into one's own language of the sacred text ["The Task of the Translator," in _Illuminations_]. A sacred text is untranslatable, says Benjamin, precisely because the meaning and the letter cannot be dissociated. The flow of meaning and the flow of literality cannot be dissociated, thus the sacred text is untranslatable. The only thing one can do when translating a sacred text is to read between the lines, between its lines. Benjamin says that this reading or this intralinear version of the sacred text is the ideal of all translation: pure translatability. Here, then, we are dealing with a sacred text in the sense that it is irreducibly tied to a language, to a proper name which can belong to only one language and can desire its translation into only one language. Babel equals Confusion. This is the paradigm of the situation in which there is a multiplicity of languages and in which translation is both necessary and impossible. At that very moment, it performs the situation it describes; in other words, the name of God here is, at the same time, the name of all proper names. They are all in a state of Babel; in all of them the desire is at work to impose the proper name with the demand: "Translate me and don't translate me." If we could read Benjamin's text together, we would see that this requirement, this demand, this wretchedness of the proper name, crying after its translation even as it makes it impossible—"translate me but, what-

---

*Derrida condenses at least four senses in this invented word: dissemination, deschematization, de-"Shemitizing," and derouting or diverting from a path (the word _chemin_ meaning path or road).—Tr.

ever you do, don't translate me"—all of this is of an absolutely general order. This generalized singularity is what the Babel account describes.

Just a few more words on this subject. In the latest French translation of the Babel story, [the translator] Chouraqui's language tries to be poetic and as literal as possible. But there comes a moment when he is obliged to write: Bavel. Then, however, he hesitates over whether or not to translate into French the meaning audible to the Shems in the original text. He has to make the French ear hear that it means confusion, but he is unable to do it in a way that is internal to his translation, that is, a way that isn't an analysis or a clarification. So what he does is to write: "Bavel, Confusion," capitalizing Confusion. In the language of the original text, there is only one word, whereas the translation has recourse to two words. But the translator realizes that without the capital letter, he loses the effect of a proper name. He thus arrives at this manner of compromise, which, naturally, is insufficient, but which has been forced on him by God's deconstruction.

This inscribes the scene of translation within a scene of inheritance and in a space which is precisely that of the genealogy of proper names, of the family, the law, indebtedness. Obviously, one can see the question of the father, which you asked at the end of your remarks, taking shape here. At a certain moment you made allusion to the "*tranche-fert*," but I fear this allusion may have remained unclear for those who are unfamiliar with the very specific context in which that word was put forward. Perhaps I'll say a few words about it so that it will no longer be such a secret. The expression *tranche-fert* is one I ventured to put before some French psychoanalysts during a working session I had with them. What I wanted to indicate with this word is what is called the *tranche*.* I don't know if the same word is used in Quebec, but in France the *tranche* is that analysis psychoanalysts sometimes do for a while with a colleague. That is, an analyst who is settled into

---

*Piece, slice, from *trancher*: to slice, separate, decide. The play is on the psychoanalytic term *transfert*: transference.—Tr.

the analytic profession, who is certified as an analyst and practices analysis, at some point deems it necessary for whatever reason to return for another little bit of analysis with a colleague. This is what is called a _tranche._ Well, sometimes this second analyst—or the third or the fourth one—to whom he or she goes belongs to another psychoanalytic group. As you know, in France there are at least four groups within the analytic establishment, and the fact of going from one analyst to another or from one group to another—sometimes also from one sex to another (from a man analyst to a woman analyst or the other way around)—poses a certain number of problems on different levels which I think are important. It was in order to pose the problem of transference entailed in this situation that I played with the word "_tranche-fert,_" which Patrick Mahony referred to.

Before getting to what you said about the concept of translation in Freud—and I don't want to keep the floor too long—I would like to venture a word on the subject of the history of names in one's life. As you have already said, we have a series of names throughout our lives. We are constantly being named by different names which add up, disappear, accumulate, and so on. But what one may well ask oneself is whether, beneath the proper name or names that are in one way or another public knowledge, there does not exist a proper name that is unconscious and secret, a name we are in search of or that the reader or analyst must seek out. For example, to pick up on what Claude Lévesque was saying yesterday, reading a dismembered or disseminated proper name in a text can sometimes be an interesting, more or less difficult exercise, a more or less fascinating piecing together of clues. But it can also be a total trap. In effect, once one has reconstituted, for example, the name of Francis Ponge* disseminated in his text, once one has explained all the rules of this dismembering and this monumentalization, perhaps one has gotten off on altogether the wrong track. And this because Francis Ponge has perhaps a secret or unconscious name which has nothing at all to do

---

*See _Signéponge/Signsponge_ where Derrida works out a reading of Ponge's signature in and on his work.—Tr.

with either Francis or Ponge. Perhaps all of the poetic work he does in order to mark his patronym in his text, either in pieces or in an integral fashion, is a means not only of misleading the reader or the detectives—the critical detectives—but also of losing himself. Perhaps he doesn't know his proper name. Is it possible not to know one's own name? In any case, this is the question you wanted to ask: Is it possible for the unconscious proper name—that to which the other addresses him/herself in us, that which responds in us—to be secret? Can there be unconscious proper names, names that are at work in the whole psychic organization, the whole topical structure? Can such a name exist? It is difficult already to formulate and support the hypothesis that there exists such a first name, before the name, a kind of absolutely secret first name which functions all the time without our knowing it. (All of a sudden, when a certain appeal is made either by some voice, some tongue, some gesture, or some kind of scene, I respond to it because it touches my secret desire—that is, my proper name.) But let us nevertheless put the hypothesis forward. Let's suppose I have a secret proper name that has nothing to do with my public proper name or with what anyone may know about me. Suppose also that from time to time some other may call me by this secret proper name, either by uttering certain words or syllables or by making certain gestures or signs. (The secret proper name, the absolute idiom, is not necessarily on the order of language in the phonic sense but may be on the order of a gesture, a physical association, a scene of some sort, a taste, a smell. And it is to this appeal that I would essentially respond, this call that would command me absolutely.) My proper name may be associated with—I don't know—let's say a scent, to take the easiest hypothesis. It would be enough to present me with it in a certain situation in order to call me by this scent. This, then, could be the secret name.

Although our hypothesis is a difficult one, I would like to express certain reservations as to this hypothesis itself. I think it's necessary to formulate it, but one must also be aware that,

however daring it might be, it nevertheless presumes the possibility of some absolute properness, an absolute idiom. However, if an idiom effect or an effect of absolute properness can
arise only within a system of relations and differences with
something else that is either near or far, then the secret proper
name is right away inscribed—structurally and a priori—in a
network where it is contaminated by common names. Thus,
even this secret proper name would be impossible, at least in
a pure state. There may be effects of a secret proper name, but
they could not possibly occur in a pure state because of the
differential structure of any mark. This secret mark could be
what it is only in a relation of differentiation and thus also of
contamination, in a network or common system. It would give
up its secret, then, at the very moment in which it would have
the best and closest hold on it. If this absolute secret cannot
exist in the strictest purity, I can never be assured that an
appeal is addressed to me. You spoke of the *address:* you said
that in analysis there should come a moment when the analyst
addresses the patient by his/her name. This may be very difficult, very lengthy, very improbable, but, finally, the ideal pole
or conclusion of analysis would be the possibility of address-
ing the patient using his or her most proper name, possibly
the most secret. It is the moment, then, when the analyst
would say to the patient "you" in such a way that there would
be no possible misunderstanding on the subject of this "you."
Well, if what I have just said is at all pertinent, that is, if the
most secret proper name has its effect of a proper name only
by risking contamination and detour within a system of relations, then it follows that pure address is impossible. I can
never be sure when someone says to me—or to you—says to
me, "you, you," that it might not be just any old "you." I can
never be sure that the secret address might not be diverted,
like any message or letter, so that it does not arrive at its
destination. This is inscribed in the most general structure of
the mark. The proper name is a mark: something like confusion can occur at any time because the proper name bears
confusion within itself. The most secret proper name is, up to

a certain point, synonymous with confusion. To the extent to which it can immediately become common and drift off course toward a system of relations where it functions as a common name or mark, it can send the address off course. The address is always delivered over to a kind of chance, and thus I cannot be assured that an appeal or an address is addressed to whom it is addressed. There are, then, aleatory or chance elements at work in every kind of message, every type of letter, all mail, if you will.

I am going on too long, so I will try to accelerate things a bit. As for psychoanalysis, everything Freud tells us about translation, all the uses he makes of translation, may in part appear to be metaphorical as regards the common concept of translation, which is what Jakobson calls interlinguistic translation, or translation in the everyday sense. Freud, on the other hand, very often, as in the examples you gave, also speaks of translation as the passage from one semiotic system to another. When one speaks of hysteria, of oneiric or hysterical translation, one is speaking of translation in Jakobson's third sense, the passage from one semiotic system to another: words–gestures, words–images, acoustic–visual, and so forth. but to the extent that Freud seems to want to use the word "translation" in a metaphorical sense, he constantly looks as if he is taking the literal sense (that is, interlinguistic translation) as the model referent for all possible translation. Here we see how the linguisticistic temptation can inhabit psychoanalysis. I don't think Freud gives in to this temptation very much; but, without a doubt, [Jacques] Lacan gives in to it—that is, he everywhere engages in it in the most forceful and the most systematic manner, which one may judge from the fact that it is the linguistic body or linguistic rhetoric which organizes all the other translating transformations. In Lacan, the linguistic code, the spoken code, has a dominant role over the other codes and other transformations which, in a certain way, can all be translated into language by means of translation in the linguistic sense. This is a very serious problem and I can only evoke it here. It is, however, inevitable whenever one speaks of these different meanings of the word "translation."

I want to say a few words on the subject of anasemia. It is an easy transition to make, I think, after what has just been said about Lacan or linguisticism, and I would also add about logocentrism and phallogocentrism. You very lucidly isolated that one little sentence in my introduction to Nicolas Abraham on the subject of the anasemic translation of Freud's statement according to which the libido is essentially virile. The phrase is Abraham's. He tries to demonstrate that when Freud says that all libido is essentially virile (with all the consequences that that might have within his system, but we can't go into that here), this must be heard and understood anasemically. That is, it must not be taken literally but understood according to what Abraham calls anasemia: the return toward concepts which are not only originary but pre-originary, which are, in other words, on this side of meaning. Briefly, Abraham explains that when psychoanalysis talks about Pleasure, for example, or about Ego, it capitalizes these words in order, for one thing, to translate words that, like all German substantives, are capitalized in Freud's text. However, according to Abraham, when Freud talks of this or that major analytic concept, he does not intend them in the ordinary sense of the language. Thus, Pleasure does not mean what one understands by pleasure. Rather, Pleasure is that on the basis of which the meaning of pleasure can be determined. This is to say that one must go back to this side of meaning (thus, the sense or direction of the word "anasemia") in order to understand how meaning has been formed. On what conditions is there pleasure? On what conditions does the word "pleasure" have a meaning? On that condition which Freud calls Pleasure in his metapsychology and which has an anasemic sense; therefore it is capitalized. Thus, it is on the basis of this system or this theory of anasemia (it is, I remind you, Nicolas Abraham's theory, and I am only commenting on it in my own manner in the text you cite) that Freud's statement according to which all libido is virile, even in the woman, does not signify what one may understand in general when this statement is made in everyday language. It does not signify, that is, the primacy or the privilege of the phallus, but rather that basis on which there can be a phallus or libido. In my opinion, the problem remains intact. I claim no responsibility here, nor can I go into this problem because of the lack of time.

I would say just one final word about patricide. Obviously, the idea that everything I do is of a patricidal nature, as the texts you cited say or as you yourself have said, is an idea that only half pleases me. It's not wrong, but if it were essentially that or only that, I would be very disappointed. Of course I agree that there is patricide in it—in a certain way patricide is inevitable—but I also try to do something else which, in my opinion, cannot be understood simply within the scene of patricide that is so recurrent and so imitable. Thus, if you were trying to suggest that what I do might be in some way inimitable as, for instance, in patricide, well, I would have to say that nothing is more imitable than patricide and therefore nothing is more often repeated. If, for the reason I mentioned at the beginning, the manner in which I write—but the same goes for anyone—has something barely imitable about it (I don't believe that there is anything inimitable, so let's say barely imitable), it would be to the extent that something were not of a patricidal nature, because nothing is more imitable than patricide. However, I don't believe in the inimitable any more than I believe in the secret and absolutely pure proper name.

Rodolphe Gasché: *The Operator of Differance**

Before getting to my questions, I want to make a preliminary remark. The invitation I received to participate in this round-table on translation cannot be explained—or at least I don't imagine that it can—only by the fact that I translated your *Writing and Difference* into German and thus into a language which is not, any more than the other ones I use, my mother tongue. So that it won't be a secret, I will tell you that my mother tongue is double—Flemish and Luxembourgish. Two

*See above, p. xii, on this word.

dialects, therefore, between which, for better or worse, I have had to and have managed to situate myself. Thus, the fact that I have been asked to participate in this discussion is not completely determined by the translation problems that I may have encountered with the German transposition of _Writing and Difference_. It is also, I hope, overdetermined by this double aspect of my mother tongue as well as by the translation problem which that implies from the very beginning. (I note here, right away, that this bilingualism does not necessarily bring with it any kind of mastery in the matter of translation. On the contrary, as my translation readily demonstrates.)

Jacques Derrida, I remember that several years ago, you said to me (permit me this indiscretion if it is one) that you were writing _against_ the French language, more precisely against the institutionalized language of the metropolis, which was not, strictly speaking, your mother tongue. Let me then set this statement in a border alongside your life and your "works" (if, once again, I may permit myself such an expression) and open your texts and your writing to the question of this double relation to your mother tongue. It is, then, a mother tongue that is yours without really being yours and whose duplicity you take on. The day before yesterday, you spoke of autobiography in this strong sense of the term, and it is in this sense that again today I would like to interrogate the problematic developed, for example, in "Me—Psychoanalysis," your introduction to the English translation of Abraham's "The Shell and the Kernel." It seems to me that what interests you first of all in the work of this psychoanalyst is the idea of a fissure or a crack in the very notion of the maternal tongue (and, thinking of your text "Du Tout" ["Of the Whole"], I would add in the maternal language of the psychoanalytic institution in France as well). You then remark the double translation that occurs de facto in any maternal tongue. You illustrate this, on the one hand, with the phenomenological reduction of language to its intentional meaning carried out by Abraham and, on the other hand, by the asemic translation of psychoanalysis which, from the asemic agency of the unconscious, questions the very phenomenality of meaning. You then show that this double translation operating within the same language precedes anything called "translation" in a phenomenological sense. This double translation operating in the very place of the mother tongue and contaminating it in such a way that it becomes a heterogeneous space is not only the condition of possibility for all translation into another language, a foreign language or the language of the other. In effect, this double translation disrupting the unity of the mother tongue is not simply a symmetrical translation because, contrary to the phenomenological reduction, psychoanalytic discourse, according to Abraham, returns to the asemic possibility of the very meaning of language assumed by phenomenological discourse. In other words, psychoanalysis, at its most radical, would account in this way for the very possibility of translation as it operates in its other or counterpart—here, in phenomenology. However, it accounts for it in a singular fashion by mining, in effect, the dissymmetry between the two originary translations. In this dialogue (if that is what it is), only psychoanalysis forces language to speak the nonlanguage conditions of speech. As you show quite well, this opens psychoanalysis, de jure, to a reapplication of its *corpus juris*, that is, the set of concepts operative in its own discourse, in psychoanalysis itself. Hence your question in this case about the Ego or the "me" of psychoanalysis.

I'll conclude rapidly before asking my questions. Not only does all translation into a foreign language rest on the very possibility of the double translation already at work in any language, but all translation of whatever sort is "rooted" in the asemic by the very dissymmetry of this double translation and therefore in that which cannot legitimately function as a "root": in the nonlanguage conditions of language. Hence the following three questions:

First question: What has been called, in reference to your work, the indetermination of any translation, you yourself have conceived (I won't say *exclusively*) against Heidegger's theory of translation and of language. I will permit myself to summarize here (but, given the circumstances, it will be an altogether imperfect summary) the way I understand Heidegger on this point. The denaturation which takes place between Greek and Latin (and, as a later result, German) represents not only a distortion or historical accident, but is also most importantly a historical destiny. This is because the distorting translation of Greek concepts into the Latin tongue derives from an "unthought" of the Greek language itself (that which, for example, makes possible the advent of modern technique as well as the *Ge-stell* [frame], insofar as it is an unthought of Greek thought concerning the notion of *thesis*). This explains, moreover, Heidegger's refusal of a nostalgic return to the Greeks. For him, it is at most a question of returning—if it can be called a return—to something that can be envisioned only through the Greeks and that takes shape as the *Heim* [home] to come. Thus, the Heideggerian return cannot be a return to the Greek mother tongue (and to Greek thought), but to something before the Greek mother tongue, to something already at work in it, cracking it apart, and which it renders only imperfectly. It is a return to a mother tongue that has perhaps never taken place but that is, for Heidegger, the place we already occupy, still without knowing it. Consequently, my question shapes up as follows: How do you situate yourself in relation to Heidegger's at least implicit recognition of a fundamental lack in every mother tongue, in this case the Greek language, but also in every language in general?

My second question is a question by circumlocution. Do you speak the *same* French as the French do, or do you rather translate French in the direction of an asemic kernel which is French's other within itself? What, then, is the relation—if there is one—of this other French within French to the German language?

Finally, my third question, which is more general. If, as you have indeed shown in "Fors," any translation, of whatever sort, has its starting point in the impossible translation of each language's asemic kernel—a kernel that is obviously nonidentical and nonpresent to itself—does translation leave it intact as an unrepresentable kernel or, on the contrary, does every translation only help to better displace and better defer the absolute nonpresence of this kernel itself? Or to put it still more simply, isn't translation the operator of differance, deferring and differing that which makes it possible? And in this case, shouldn't we instead take up the problem again of the conditions of possibility of any translation and of its effect—namely, differance?

Jacques Derrida: *Reply*

These very difficult questions are very lucidly formulated, there where it is quite certain and clear that I cannot respond. Therefore, thank you. I am going to see if there is not among them some common kernel. And I believe there is one: it is, precisely, the "kernel." The question is whether there is a kernel intact somewhere or other. When Heidegger, in your reading of him, assumes that behind the Greek language itself—that language which the Romans, for example, are supposed to have forgotten, disfigured, and mistranslated—there is another language, an "unthought" for the Greeks themselves of their own language, he presupposes something like an archi-originary intactness that has been basically forgotten in advance, immediately covered over with oblivion from the first, for example by the Greeks. This explains, in effect, Heidegger's remark that we should avoid interpreting his text, according to a well-known motif of German thought, as a nostalgic return to Greece. Nevertheless, if it is not a question of returning in the direction of the Greek language, it is at least necessary to presuppose something absolutely forgotten and always dissimulated in advance behind the Greek language—an arch–mother tongue, a grandmother tongue, a granny of the Greek language who would be absolutely virginal: an untouchable, virgin granny. This motif of the untouchable is not insignificant. One also finds it in Benjamin's text where we read that translation cannot "touch" or attain something. There is something "untouchable," something of the original text that no translation can attain. Two of Benjamin's metaphors in this regard intersect in a curious fashion with the central metaphor of "The Shell and the Kernel." The kernel of the original text is untouchable by the translation, and this untouchable something is the sacred, which says: Don't touch me. Thus, for Heidegger there would also be something untouchable. Translation, in the sense Heidegger gives to this word, is no longer simply a linguistic operation that consists in transporting meaning from one language to another. He says somewhere that it is an operation of thought through which we must translate ourselves into the thought of the other language, the forgotten thinking of the other language. We must translate ourselves into it and not make it come into our language. It is necessary to go toward the unthought thinking of the other language. Let's suppose that there is an untouchable kernel and that we must presume its permanence without hoping to make it come simply into our language. When you ask me, coming now to your second question, if I speak the same French as the French do, this question presupposes that there is a French language I circle around, do violence to, write against, transform, and so on. It presupposes that there is a body of pure French which I seek to violate or to appropriate to myself and in relation to which I will determine myself. It would be this body of pure French which makes the law and in relation to whose law I define myself. Finally, the intact kernel is directly implied in your third question.

Well, I can't answer all these questions in a serious, analytic fashion. It seems to me that, if I were able to work out a response, the diagram I would follow would be roughly like this: The desire for the intact kernel is desire itself, which is to say that it is irreducible. There is a prehistoric, preoriginary relation to the intact kernel, and it is only beginning with this relation that any desire whatsoever can constitute itself. Thus, the desire or the _phantasm_ of the intact kernel is irreducible— despite the fact that _there is no_ intact kernel. I would oppose desire to necessity, to _anankē_. The _anankē_ is that there is no intact kernel and there never has been one. That's what one wants to forget, and to forget that one has forgotten it. It's not that something has been forgotten; rather, one wants to forget that there is nothing to forget, that there has been nothing to forget. But one can only forget that there has never been an intact kernel. This phantasm, this desire for the intact kernel sets in motion every kind of desire, every kind of tongue, appeal, address. This is the necessity and it's a hard one, a terrible necessity. But just as without the desire for the intact kernel which doesn't exist, the desire for the untouchable, for virginity (the taboo on virginity has an essential relation to all this)—just as without this desire for virginity no desire whatever would be set moving, likewise without Necessity and without what comes along to interrupt and thwart that desire, desire itself would not unfold. I don't know what else to call this but Necessity with a capital N, something that no one can do anything about and that is not a law instituted by any subject. Without this Necessity, it's law against law, desire against desire, proper name against proper name. But there is a law above these laws, which I am calling *anankē* and which controls it all (in this way, perhaps, I think in Greek, more in Greek than in Jewish). Thus, above the scene of the war between Yahweh and the Shemites, there is *anankē*, that is, a law which is not produced by any desire but which controls the struggle between these desires and these proper names. This *anankē*, no less than the desire for virginity, is what makes possible the kernel desire itself—the intact desire for intactness.

Christie V. McDonald: *The Passage into Philosophy*

In "Plato's Pharmacy," you stated: "To a considerable degree, we have already said all we *meant to say.* . . . With the exception of this or that supplement, our questions will have nothing more to name but the texture of the text, reading and writing, mastery and play, the paradoxes of supplementarity, and the graphic relations between the living and the dead." You added that the strange logic of the term "*pharmakon*," which is translated as both "remedy" and "poison," would from then on be linked to what you called the problem of translation in which one would "be dealing with nothing less than the problem of the very passage into philosophy."

My remarks today concern the relationship between reading and writing, a relationship which seems to have been taking shape in your work for a long time now in terms of translation considered as an enterprise that is at once possible and impossible. In *Spurs*, one finds a single text dispersed across the page, which is divided into four columns, each one a translation into a different language by a different translator. As a result, any question of translation becomes right away a problem of reading. If meaning remains intact from one language to another, is transmissible and susceptible to a legitimate operation of readability (in teaching, for example), it is because it first of all conforms to the rule according to which a good translation follows the internal logic of what is called the "original." At the same time, however, this meaning is dispersed by the excessive play within the historical and semantic transference of languages. In *Glas*, reading is also fractured by the columns and other elements at play (such as the etymologies and the explanations set apart on the page), but this fragmentation no longer translates a (so-called) same text.

I would therefore like to raise once more the question that returns *both* in the text entitled "Living On" *and* in its companion or mate (its shipmate, so to speak): the log.* This ques-

---

*Here is how this text is laid out typographically: At the bottom of the page, running the length of the text entitled "Living On" and accompanying it, a note, another text is inscribed which has the title "Borderlines" [*Journal de bord*: ship's journal or log]. Both were written by Jacques Derrida and both were meant from the first to be translated. The wager is the following: The note, "Borderlines," written in a stenotelegraphic style, tends (by principle and by contract) toward the greatest possible translatability. "Living On," on the other hand, which is the chief or principal text, puts into motion an enigmatic and disjointed writing where the "unrepresentable" is in force—and this, precisely, by means of the *récit* or the performative. These two texts play at the limits of the everyday concept of translation: the note cannot be totally translatable ("totally translatable," says the narrator, "it disappears as a text"); just as "Living On" cannot remain completely untranslatable ("totally

tion is the following: How, in effect, does one text read another? By proposed contract, your ship's log—"Borderlines"—
promises, just like some translating language or translator
metalanguage, to aim for the greatest possible translatability.
Be that as it may, it nevertheless tends toward a distortion of
the initial contract, and in the end you say as much. You do
not keep your promise, since the double band reproduces the
supplementary trait of this structure and gives rise to a lesson
(to your translators). This lesson is not in the form of a revela-
tion of a paradigm, but rather of a cross-reference to the network of texts which are living by means of what you call
"living on" [sur-vie], and living on only because they are at
once translatable and untranslatable. You say that if you are
continuing to speak of "texts" instead of making reference to a
differential network, an indefinite movement of traces referring back to other differential traces, it is partly for strategic
reasons. I wonder if the force of this strategy does not come
from maintaining divisions that are always both arbitrary and
nonarbitrary. I say this because it seems to me that writing—in
the sense you give to the term—draws at least part of its con-
testatory force from that which it contests: the institution.
Benjamin writes: "There is no muse of philosophy, nor is
there one of translation. But despite the claims of sentimental
artists, these two are not banausic. For there is a philosophical
genius that is characterized by a yearning for that language
which manifests itself in translations." Just as one could propose, as Claude Lévesque did yesterday, that Derrida is to be
found somewhere "*derrière le rideau*" in the *fort/da*, making
allusion to the text entitled "Freud's Legacy," couldn't one

---

untranslatable . . . the text dies immediately"). Although the typographic fron-
tier between the note and the text seems clear cut, one comes to realize that it
is destined to be constantly overrun. The same is true of its corollary: the
division which is marked between *the critical* (the translating metalanguage
of the note) and *the deconstructive* (the play of writing in "Living On," which
overflows in the direction of dissemination). It is, moreover, the coupling of
the terms "deconstruction" and "criticism" that gives the whole volume its
title.

also propose the hypothesis that, in the series of couples ("Living On/Borderlines"; *The Triumph of Life/Death Sentence;* the narrator and the woman in Blanchot's *Death Sentence;* and, finally, the most extraordinary couple of all, the two women separated by the partitioning of the two parts of the latter text), one finds, in a certain manner, the staging of the possibility and impossibility of writing in the notion of reading as an act of translation? In the same text already mentioned, Benjamin writes:

Fragments of an amphora which are to be glued together must match one another in the smallest details, although they need not be like one another. In the same way a translation, instead of resembling the meaning of the original, must lovingly and in detail incorporate the original's mode of signification, thus making both the original and the translation recognizable as fragments of a greater language, just as fragments are part of an amphora.

As an instituting rule, I was taught at school to avoid what were called false friends, that is, a word that is the same in two languages but whose meaning is different. In an altogether different context, might one not suggest to you the following, slightly mad hypothesis: Your remark in "Living On" about the two women who, perhaps, love each other across the partition of the two parts of the text—these two aphonic voices telephoning each other, just like your two texts which communicate only by telegraph—takes up a position analogous to that of false friends doing what one must not do on the basis of an unconscious and imperceptible structure of the *récit*. Among all these *récits*, yours as well as those of Blanchot, that interrogate so radically the hermeneutic process of interpretation, what has become of that translation problem announced as the program in "Plato's Pharmacy"—the problem of the passage into philosophy?

Jacques Derrida: *Reply*

The program of the passage into philosophy signifies in this context, it seems to me, that the philosophical operation, if it has an originality and specificity, defines itself as a project of translation. More precisely, it defines itself as the fixation of a certain concept and project of translation. What does philosophy say? Let's imagine that it's possible to ask such a question: What does philosophy say? What does the philosopher say when he is being a philosopher? He says: What matters is truth or meaning, and since meaning is before or beyond language, it follows that it is translatable. Meaning has the commanding role, and consequently one must be able to fix its univocality or, in any case, to master its plurivocality. If this plurivocality can be mastered, then translation, understood as the transport of a semantic content into another signifying form, is possible. There is no philosophy unless translation in this latter sense is possible. Therefore the thesis of philosophy is translatability in this common sense, that is, as the transfer of a meaning or a truth from one language to another without any essential harm being done. Obviously, this project or this thesis has taken a certain number of forms which one could locate throughout the history of philosophy from Plato to Hegel, passing by way of [Gottfried Wilhelm] Leibnitz. This, then, was what I thought of as the passage into philosophy, the program of translation. The origin of philosophy is translation or the thesis of translatability, so that wherever translation in this sense has failed, it is nothing less than philosophy that finds itself defeated. This is precisely what I tried to deal with in "Plato's Pharmacy" by means of a certain number of words such as *pharmakon,* whose body is in itself a constant challenge to philosophy. Philosophical discourse cannot master a word meaning two things at the same time and which therefore cannot be translated without an essential loss. Whether one translates *pharmakon* as "poison" or "remedy," whether one comes down on the side of sickness or health, life or death, the undecidability is going to be lost. So, *pharmakon* is one of the limits, one of the verbal forms—but one could cite many others and many other forms—marking the limit of philosophy as translation.

I noticed that when Benjamin, in the first passage you read, speaks of philosophical genius, he makes use of a word that does not belong to his language: "*ingenium*." In the French translation of Benjamin, Maurice de Gandillac notes at the bottom of the page: " 'ingenium,' Latin word meaning, et cetera." In other words, he was obliged to translate a word Benjamin left in Latin. Right after "*ingenium*," there is the [Stéphane] Mallarmé text in French, which Benjamin does not translate because he knows that Mallarmé is untranslatable. These utterances of Mallarmé that say Babel, utterances I cannot reconstitute by heart, these superb texts speak the Babelian situations: "ces *langues imparfaites en cela que plusieurs, et cetera*."* This syntax is untranslatable and Benjamin knows it, so he leaves Mallarmé's language intact in his own text. The result is that when Gandillac translates Benjamin into French and leaves Mallarmé once again intact, this latter Mallarmé is no longer the same. Benjamin left it intact in a German context, but by reproducing it in the French translation one reproduces another example of the situation mentioned above.

Since we are talking about "Living On" (I don't know whether I will come back to the text to which I gave that title; I would rather insist on what Benjamin calls "living on" in his own text and which is a central concept there), it happens that Benjamin says substantially that the structure of an original is survival, what he calls "*Überleben*." A text is original insofar as it is a thing, not to be confused with an organic or a physical body, but a thing, let us say, of the mind, meant to survive the death of the author or the signatory, and to be above or beyond the physical corpus of the text, and so on. The structure of the original text is survival. Here, Benjamin has recourse to a certain number of Hegelian-type sentences to explain why one must understand life—"*Leben*"—not on the basis of what we know in general about organic, biological life, but, on the contrary, on the basis of the life of the mind, that is, life that rises above nature and is in its essence survi-

---

*"These imperfect tongues, imperfect in that they are several . . ."—Tr.

val. To understand a text as an original is to understand it independently of its living conditions—the conditions, obviously, of its author's life—and to understand it instead in its *surviving* structure. At times he says "*Überleben*" and at other times "*Fortleben*." These two words do not mean the same thing ("*Überleben*" means above life and therefore survival as something rising above life; "*Fortleben*" means survival in the sense of something prolonging life), even though they are translated in French by the one word "*survivre*" [to survive, to live on], which already poses a problem. Given the *surviving* structure of an original text—always a sacred text in its own way insofar as it is a pure original—the task of the translator is precisely to respond to this demand for survival which is the very structure of the original text. (Notice Benjamin does not say the task of translation but rather of the translator, that is, of a subject who finds him/herself immediately indebted by the existence of the original, who must submit to its law and who is duty-bound to do something for the original.) To do this, says Benjamin, the translator must neither reproduce, represent, nor copy the original, nor even, essentially, care about *communicating* the meaning of the original. Translation has nothing to do with reception or communication or information. As Christie McDonald has just pointed out, the translator must assure the survival, *which is to say the growth,* of the original. Translation augments and modifies the original, which, insofar as it is living on, never ceases to be transformed and to grow. It modifies the original even as it also modifies the translating language. This process—transforming the original as well as the translation—is the translation contract between the original and the translating text. In this contract it is a question of neither representation nor reproduction nor communication; rather, the contract is destined to assure a survival, not only of a corpus or a text or an author but of languages. Benjamin explains that translation reveals in some way the kinship of languages—a kinship that is not to be conceived in the manner of historical linguistics or on the basis of hypotheses about language families, and so forth. It is a kinship of another order, as Benjamin explains several times. One must not think about the life or the survival of a work on the basis of what we believe to be life in general, nor about the kinship of the families of languages on the basis of what we believe to be kinship or families in general. On the contrary, it is on the basis of languages and relations among languages that one must begin to understand what "life" and "kinship" mean. How, then, can translation assure the growth— what he calls "the hallowed growth"—of languages and the kinship among languages? By trying to fulfill that impossible contract to reconstitute, not the original, but the larger ensemble that, precisely, is gathered together here in the metaphor of the amphora—the "metamphora." That is, as in any *symbolon*, as in any symbolic system, it is a question of reconstituting a whole on the basis of fragments that became separated at the moment of the agreement, both of the parties taking a piece of the *symbolon* into their keeping. What one must try to do is to reconstitute a *symbolon*, a symbolic alliance or wedding ring between languages, but reconstitute it in such a way that the whole of the *symbolon* will be greater than the original itself and, of course, than the translation itself. However, this simple growth of languages, which aims to complete and extend each language, supposes its own limit: the sacred text.

This impossible possibility nevertheless holds out the promise of the reconciliation of tongues. Hence the messianic character of translation. The event of a translation, the performance of all translations, is not that they succeed. A translation never succeeds in the pure and absolute sense of the term. Rather, a translation succeeds in promising success, in promising reconciliation. There are translations that don't even manage to promise, but a good translation is one that enacts that performative called a promise with the result that through the translation one sees the coming shape of a possible reconciliation among languages. It is then that one has the sense or the presentiment of what language itself is—"*die reine Sprache*." Pure language, says Benjamin, is not one which has been purified of anything; rather, it is what makes a language a language, what makes for the fact that there is language. A translation puts us not in the presence but in the presentiment of what "pure language" is, that is, the fact that there is language, that language is language. This is what we learn from a translation, rather than the meaning contained in the translated text, rather than this or that particular meaning. We learn that there is language, that language is of language, and that there is a plurality of languages which have that kinship with each other coming from their being languages. This is what Benjamin calls pure language, "*die reine Sprache,*" the being-language of language. The promise of a translation is that which announces to us this being-language of language: there is language, and because there is something like language, one is both able and unable to translate.

One more remark, but it is neither an answer nor a commentary—just a freestyle gloss on *Death Sentence*. It happens that in *Death Sentence* one of the two women dies. As you know, the book is divided into two absolutely or apparently independent *récits*. In each case, the narrator (but it is not even certain that the one who says "I" is the same in both parts) has formed a couple—a very curious couple—with a woman. Let's just leave it at that. In the second case, the woman happens to be a translator, and he has a relation to her that is curious in many respects, only one of which I need mention here. She is a translator whose mother tongue is a foreign language—a Slavic language—that he doesn't know very well. When, from time to time, he wants to say irresponsible things to her, things that, as he says, do not put him under any obligation— when he wants to have fun or say foolish things to her that are not binding on him—he speaks to her in her language. At that moment he is irresponsible, because it is the other's language. He can say anything at all, since he does not assume responsibility for what he says. (Or, to come back to Rodolphe Gasché's question, let's say that when I speak French, I am perhaps washing my hands of everything I say because it isn't my tongue; if one is not responsible when one speaks the other's tongue, one is let off the hook in advance.) One finds oneself in the following paradoxical situation, which also seems to me to be paradigmatic: You can only enter into a contract, a hymen, an essential alliance, if you do so in your own tongue. You're only responsible, in other words, for what you say in your own mother tongue. If, however, you say it only in your own tongue, then you're still not committed, because you must also say it in the other's language. An agreement or obligation of whatever sort—a promise, a marriage, a sacred alliance—can only take place, I would say, in translation, that is, only if it is *simultaneously* uttered in both my tongue and the other's. If it takes place in only one tongue, whether it be mine or the other's, there is no contract possible. When the narrator speaks to her, a translator, in her language, Slavic, he is not responsible: he can say anything whatever and it is not binding on him. If he wanted to speak only in his tongue, she would not be bound either, and she would not acknowledge receipt. In order for the contract or the alliance to take place, in order for the "yes, yes" to take place on both sides, it must occur in two languages at once. Now, one may think of these two languages "at once" as being two national languages, for example French and Slavic, and that's the easiest way to understand it. But it can also be two tongues within the same language, for example your French and my French, which are obviously not the same. Thus, the agreement, the contract in general, has to imply the difference of languages rather than transparent translatability, a Babelian situation which is at the same time lessened and left intact. If one can translate purely and simply, there is no agreement. And if one can't translate at all, there is no agreement either. In order for there to be an agreement, there has to be a Babelian situation, so that what I would call the translation contract—in the transcendental sense of this term, let's say—is the contract itself. Every contract must be a translation contract. There is no contract possible—no social contract possible—without a translation contract, bringing with it the paradox I have just mentioned. To continue, then, in *Death Sentence* the extraordinary situation of these two women, who perhaps draw up a secret contract between themselves and not only with the narrator, is at work in the contract as I have just described it. This complicates the situation infinitely, but I think one must refer to it.

The expression "false friends," which you cited, exists in French as well, but there is another expression in the everyday code of translation. In school, as one says, one had to be on one's guard also against *"belles infidèles"* [beautiful, faithless ones]. These *belles infidèles* are the same as false friends, that is, apparently correct translations that in fact lay a trap.

Eugenio Donato: *Specular Translation*

I am somewhat at a loss following my colleagues Rodolphe Gasché and Christie McDonald, who have already covered the ground of the several remarks I wanted to propose to you. Thus, I will be extremely brief. In fact, I am not going to ask a question, but rather will simply propose several signposts for a possible itinerary by means of certain quotations from Derrida.

Have we not in a certain way always thought—and for the reason that Jacques Derrida just gave in response to Christie McDonald—that a perfect translation, if possible, has its only possibility in the philosophic text where the text is effaced of its own accord, and that the philosopher, in the Hegelian sense, is the horizon of the literary text? The very constitution of meaning in the text would imply that there is a horizon of possible translation with a subject. In fact, I believe one should also put in question the translator–subject. We always postulate an ideal subject who will one day perhaps master the two languages and make them communicate with each other in an identity that would efface the path of the sign (or the path of the translation as the path of the sign). Hence, the whole problematic of the ground covered by translation (if it is isomorphic with the path of the sign) should fall within the critique Derrida has done of the sign in the relation of philosophy to literature and of that remainder which must always remain and inhabit every text.

From this, then, I postulate, on the one hand, that the necessity of possible translation is the necessity and the impossibility at the same time of the autotranslation of each text by itself; and, on the other hand, that translation is only the possibility of translation, only the possibility or impossibility of every text's self-speculation by itself. It will not surprise us that Hegel, for example, says in *The Aesthetics* that poetry is defined by being always translatable. It's not surprising, after Derrida's analyses of Hegel, that it would be Hegel who said that. If philosophy is translatable, poetry is all the more so, because poetry, as he defines it, is subordinated to philosophic meaning, to a "*Bedeutung*" already comprehending itself.

The second stage I wanted to propose was once again on the subject of Heidegger. I want to come back to a text of Heidegger's in order at least to suggest that, in Heidegger, the Hegelian gesture remains all the same, perhaps in spite of everything, inscribed in this problem of translation. Unfortunately, I don't have the text here, but I was thinking of that first paragraph in "*Der Spruch des Anaximander*" ["The Anaximander Fragment"], where Heidegger says more or less that, in order to speak this original speech, the original speech which speaks the origin, we must do an "*Übersetzung*," a translation, et cetera. It is interesting to note here that the word "*Übersetzung*" has a double etymology in German and thus a somewhat stronger semantic field, since one of the senses of "*Übersetzung*" (translation, metaphor, transfer) is to leap over an abyss. Thus it poses both the abyss dividing things in two and at the same time the possibility of leaping over the abyss. The text continues and in the same paragraph, beginning with this possible translation, the opposition appears between language and thought. This opposition, which is perhaps still an echo of a Hegelian problematic, is always there to the extent to which he says, "*Dichten ist denken*" ["to make poetry is to think"]. If one verifies the etymology of the word "*dichten*" in Ding's dictionary (which is justified insofar as Heidegger ventures into etymological considerations), one realizes that "*dichten*" also means "to think," and thus one remains within the circle of the opposition between "*dichten*" and "*denken*," while at the same time it comes down to the proposition "*denken ist denken*." Beginning with the problem of translation, Heidegger poses a necessary and irreconcilable doubleness, but at the same time he maintains an ambiguity in the terms that create the opposition engendering this doubleness.

Returning to the thought of Jacques Derrida, one becomes aware that the problem has been radicalized. In "Borderlines," we read:

"One never writes either in one's own language or in a foreign language. . . . *Übersetzung* and "translation" overcome, equivocally, in the course of an equivocal combat, the loss of an object. A text lives only if it lives *on*, and it lives *on* only if it is *at once* translatable *and* untranslatable (always "at once . . . and . . .': *hama*, at the same time). Totally translatable, it disappears as a text, as writing, as a body of language. Totally untranslatable, even within what is believed to be one language, it dies immediately. Thus triumphant translation is neither the life nor the death of the text, only or already its living *on*, its life after life, its life after death. The same thing will be said of what I call writing, mark, trace, and so on. It neither lives nor dies; it lives *on*. And it "starts" only with living on (testament, iterability, remaining [*restance*], crypt, detachment that lifts the strictures of the "living" *rectio* or direction of an "author" not drowned at the edge of his text).

I would thus propose quite simply that there is perhaps work to be done here if it is true that the concept of translation, such as it has been thought of in a certain philosophic tradition, is still marked by the concept of speculation. In fact, one can understand Derrida's mistrust with regard to certain concepts such as the *mise en abîme** (in "Freud's Legacy," you say that you mistrust the *mise en abîme*), since it remains within the speculative movement. Translation can be thought of as a speculative *mise en abîme* of each text. Conversely, it would be necessary to think about translation's topology in

*See above, p.62.

the completely different terms that Derrida proposes to us, that is, the possibility of _invagination_, in which nothing would remain but edges or borders.

If I may, I will conclude with a piece of whimsy. I am going to try to translate the problem of translation in function of the problematic of the dead father, the living mother, and so on. If the problem of translation is linked to the problem of the maternal tongue, thus to the living language, wouldn't the dead father in this tableau occupy the place of constituted meaning, which would only be constituted by the loss of the object, the murder of the object in that typically Hegelian gesture? If so, then, translating _invagination_ in function of the problematic of the living mother and the dead father, I wonder whether the following formulation would not be possible: The tear in the mother's living body must always give birth to and must always abort the memory of the father who is always dead.

Jacques Derrida: _Reply_

You'll have to give me time to take in that last formulation. I will simply converse with the motif of the Hegel–Heidegger dialogue. I too am aware of the possibility of a Hegelian repetition in Heidegger's discourse, but, paradoxically, instead of seeing it from the angle of philosophical translatability—or rather, instead of pulling Heidegger in the direction of Hegel— perhaps inversely one could pull Hegel in the direction of Heidegger. That is, one could remark certain utterances in Hegel concerning precisely the possibility of speculation, of speculative language and a certain number of words in the German language which Hegel says are naturally speculative and, in a certain way, untranslatable. (There's a whole list of words that Hegel used in decisive passages and about which he remarks that they belong to the good fortune of the German tongue, which is, in these particular words, naturally "speculative.") Thus, when Hegel says "_Aufhebung_" or "_Urteil_" or "_Beispiel_," he is clearly marking a certain untranslatability of these words. The word "*aufheben*" means at once to conserve and to suppress, and this double signification cannot be translated by a single word into other languages. One can interpret, one can find analogues, but one cannot translate purely and simply. At the point where the word "*Aufhebung*" is produced in the German tongue, there is something untranslatable, and far from being a limit on speculation, it is the chance for speculation. Thus, when Hegel writes "*Aufhebung*," when he makes use of "*Aufhebung*" as a word in a natural language which is supposed to be naturally speculative, at that moment one is dealing with something that goes toward Heidegger rather than Heidegger moving toward Hegel.

On the subject of "*Dichten–Denken*," Heidegger of course associates them, as you have said. But there are also texts where he says very precisely that, while "*Dichten–Denken*" go together and form a pair, they are *parallels* that never meet. They run parallel one beside the other. They are really other and can never be confused or translated one into the other. Yet, as parallel paths, "*dichten*" and "*denken*" nevertheless have a relation to each other which is such that at places they cut across each other. They are parallels that intersect, as paradoxical as that may seem. By cutting across each other, they leave a mark, they cut out a notch. And this language of the cut or break is marked in the text of Heidegger's I'm thinking of: *Unterwegs zur Sprache* [*The Way to Language*]. They do not wound each other, but each cuts across the other, each leaves its mark in the other even though they are absolutely other, one beside the other, parallel. There is also, therefore, a trend in Heidegger emphasizing the irreducibility of "*Dichten–Denken*" and thus their nonpermutability.

Forgive these remarks. If I may say so, your remarks did not call for an answer. I can only add that I will try to let your final sentence resonate.

François Péraldi: *False Sense*

Three remarks occurred to me as I was reading your introduction to Nicolas Abraham's "The Shell and the Kernel." I want to share them with you without knowing whether they will constitute a question in the proper sense or not. In effect, they tend perhaps to constitute a kind of interrogative supposition and to remain on this side of a question.

First remark: In a nice little text that has already been mentioned here, Jakobson defines the three aspects of translation: intralingual translation, interlingual translation (or translation properly speaking), and intersemiotic translation. I can't help thinking that psychoanalytic translation works like a kind of intralingual translation whose function would be the emptying out of meaning. Thus, in the passage from, or the translation of, pleasure into "pleasure" into Pleasure, which you point out in your text, the same word, pleasure, returns and "is translated into a code where it has no more meaning," the signifier remaining unchanged except for the capital letter (which is not insignificant). I was reminded here of the role of the capital letter in Charles Sanders Peirce.

Second remark: In another text where he shows how the phonetic system becomes constituted for the child according to a rigorous and quasi-universal order of implication (labials, dentals, posterior occlusives, fricatives, and—the emblem of virile speech—the apical *r*), Jakobson demonstrates—if that's the word—the validity of his little edifice by remarking that in certain cases of aphasia, the destruction of the phonic edifice follows the inverse order of its acquisition. That is, it follows a kind of reversal of the original order of implication that ends up at an ultimate and last word, the last that the aphasic can utter, a kind of "mmma-mmma, ma-ma," before sinking into the gurgling silence of complete aphasia.

Third remark: Reading your introduction, therefore, I followed with interest the order of heterogeneous conversions of the same word in the same language that arrives finally at the psychoanalytic translation. This translation itself ends up at a discourse that "using the same words (those belonging to ordinary language and those, bracketed by inverted commas, belonging to phenomenology) quotes them once more in order to say something else, something else than sense." As I read, it occurred to me that there existed in the psychoanalytic world a process that is just the reverse of this one. That is, just as aphasia manifests itself by a kind of dissolution of the phonic apparatus, a destructuring reversal of the order of implication prevailing in the acquisition of phonemes, one could say that there exists a kind of aphasia or ideological destruction of psychoanalytic discourse. This destruction, which proceeds under the auspices of what Lacan has named the SAMCDA (Mutual Aid Society Against Analytic Discourse), follows a reversal of the order of those conversions that, starting out from ordinary discourse, end up at psychoanalytic discourse, passing by way of phenomenology. This reversal is a kind of turning inside out of that translating operation which ends up at the anasemic or antisemantic terms of psychoanalytic discourse. Basically what you have then is a rephenomenalization of the discourse, a resemanticization and a reconstruction of what the psychoanalytic translation had—perhaps—deconstructed.

I would like to give an example of this process and, of course, it comes from a text by the famous "New York Trio": Heinz Hartman, Ernst Kris, and Rudolph Loewenstein. The trio, for reasons it would surely be fascinating to study, has found itself taking on the role of the collective agent (or agents) of this resemanticizing operation of the Freudian discourse at the heart of the North American psychoanalytic establishment.

In an article written in 1949 and entitled "The Theory of Aggression," the three authors confide that they don't know what to do with the Freudian theory of the death instinct, which—in other words—makes no sense in their reading of Freudian metapsychology. In effect, they say (and they are going to be playing on the register of interlingual translation in a manner that is at the very least equivocal), the *instincts*, which they distinguish from *drives*, are an object for biology, whereas drives and only drives constitute psychoanalytic notions. They oppose *aggressive drives* to the *death instinct* which, because it is an instinct, they leave to biology and to Freud's biologizing speculations.

There is a surprising translation mistake here, a false sense, to be precise. In *Beyond the Pleasure Principle*, where he introduces the question of death in a new form, Freud does not talk about a death instinct (which in German would be _Todes Instinkt_), but of _Tode Triebe_, which, strictly speaking, could only be translated as "death drives" in English. Thus, by keeping only the external manifestations (the _aggressive drives_) of this anasemic concept par excellence, our three authors have, one may say, rephenomenalized, resemanticized the psychoanalytic discourse at the very point where Freud was leading them toward one of those anasemic terms that are essential to the constitution of this psychoanalytic discourse. This divergence in the translation, this false sense, is all the more interesting in that, several pages later, the authors are careful to emphasize the difference between _drives_, which is the translation of the German _Triebe_, and _instinct_, which translates the German _Instinkt_.

The destiny of psychoanalytic discourse is being played out in this sleight of hand, this complex playing of translation effects and of meaning attributed to the translating operation. The survival of that discourse depends on what meaning will be assigned to the translation conflicts traversing it. But in what direction or what sense?

Jacques Derrida: _Reply_

Here, once again, I can acknowledge receipt but I have no response. So I'll begin by the freest association on the subject of what you said about an eventual deconstitution or a regression of psychoanalytic discourse toward a kind of aphasia, according to the well-known motif of regression: pathology as 'ression that reverses the order of acquisition and ends up at the mere proferring of "mama," the word that in some way would be at once the first to be acquired and the last in the regression. In the Joyce text I made allusion to here earlier, there is a long sequence of two very rich pages where, at the end of the terrible story of Babel, the last word is something like "mummummmum . . ." (I can't vouch for the spelling, but it's something like that). It means mama, mutism, the murmur that will not come out, the minimum of vocalization. And, obviously, it confronts the other counterpart in the paternal war. One has both the structuring of language, beginning with the father's name, and then the final, aphasic regression or the first word "mummum . . ." This is a free association on *Finnegans Wake*. It may be that the worldwide psychoanalytic establishment is on its way toward "mummum . . ."

Another association, which is a bit more than an association, concerns what you said about psychoanalytic translation as an intralingual phenomenon in the Jakobsonian sense. Yes, it's very tempting to say, for example, in the context in which Nicolas Abraham talks about anasemia (that is, in the context of metapsychology or the discourse of analytic theorization), that the word Pleasure or Unconscious is an intralingual translation of these words as they are commonly used. One translates pleasure into a homonym, Pleasure, but the homonym is already a translation of the homonym and a translating interpretation. Things no longer work quite so simply, however, when one recalls that the hypothesis of anasemia claims to return to this side of meaning. In an intralingual interpretation or translation, on the other hand, the two words or two equivalents have meaning; one explains, analyzes, or clarifies the other, but by going from meaning to meaning. It is thus a semantic operation, an operation of semantic transformation or equivalence. In anasemia, however, the capitalized word is in some way without meaning. It is before meaning, if that is possible and if Abraham is correct. The anasemic word has no meaning and does not belong to the semantic order; it is asemantic or presemantic. It is not really part of language in the sense in which the words of an intralingual transformation are all equally part of language. Moreover, according to Abraham, there is in anasemia, in analytic translation, and in the analytic use of language a kind of shift or departure from the everyday order of language which constantly dislocates the normal order of language. By means of the same words, the anasemic shift would say, not something utterly different, but rather that condition on which the everyday words of language acquire meaning. It would be a very irregular type of translation, since it would be an interpretation going back to the conditions of possibility, not of such-and-such a meaning, but of meaning in general. This anasemic reascent must be involved in order for there to be meaning. Going back toward what is preoriginary—not in the phenomenological sense of going back to the original meaning of a word, a concept, et cetera, but in this case toward the preoriginary—in this sense, it would be the fundamental translation beginning with which meaning in general could be produced. However, it would be intralingual in appearance only, that is, only according to the homonymic disguise.

Eugene Vance: *Translation in the Past Perfect*

During yesterday's discussion, Jacques Derrida spoke several times of hermeneutics in the "classical" or "traditional" sense of the term, to use his words. I have the impression that Derrida meant by that a hermeneutic tradition going back only to a relatively recent period, the one that saw the inauguration, in [Friedrich] Schleiermacher and [Wilhelm] Dilthey, of a grandoise project of understanding Understanding itself, *Verstehen* in all its majesty.

In Dilthey, *Verstehen* is the systematic return either to a kernel of original meaning occulted by the effects of time, or to a sublime meaning that can be expressed only with difficulty in "literal" terms. The privileged instrument of this hermeneutic is the science of philology.

Dilthey's reflections are situated at the dawning of the modern university, a romantic institution whose "recuperative" mandate remains more or less unchanged with two exceptions: The movements of regression have now become unthinking habits sustained by a vague feeling of nostalgia, and the quest for "origins" has come to be replaced by the quest for inert kinds of erudition. Philology, except in Germany and Italy, has lost its former speculative dimension.

To this degraded hermeneutic, Derrida wants to oppose a *keen sense of hearing*—that of the "little ear"—opening onto a new, affirmative productivity. He has made it clear to us that this is what he meant to say when in the past he used the term "deconstruction," a term he now seems to have more or less repudiated.

Everyone knows that the term "hermeneutic" has had different connotations throughout its long history. As Jean Pépin has pointed out ("L'Herméneutique ancienne," *Poétique* 23), in Greek thought the term *hermeneia* signified not so much the return, by way of exegesis, to a kernel of hidden meaning within a shell, but more the act of extroversion by the voice, the natural instrument of the soul. It is an active and prophetic productivity which is not connoted by the Latin term *interpretatio*. For the Greeks, the poetic performance of rhapsodes was a "hermeneutic" performance.

Likewise, Saint Paul will say to the Christians that it is not enough for the faithful who are possessed by God's truth to "speak in tongues." This truth must be uttered in a hermeneutic act (*diermeneuein*) that will make it comprehensible even to the uninitiated.

I am insisting on these semantic nuances in order to underscore my conviction that, when we try to delimit the motif of "translation," we are dealing with a term that has become greatly impoverished today. Among the remedies we have at our disposal is that of reinstating a semantic horizon which was much more vast at other moments of Western culture. I'm all for trying to extend as far as possible the modern concept of translation. However, our language is but the wake of a long history. And if we do not take this history into account, then the debate among "modern thinkers" may become stifling.

According to Gianfranco Folena, the French word *traduction* as well as the Italian *traduzione* are neologisms of civic humansim at the beginning of the fourteenth century.* This term displaced the terms *interpretatio* and *translatio* prevalent

---

*" 'Volgarizzare's' e 'tradurre' " in *La traduzione: Saggi e studi*, ed. centro per lo studio dell'insegnamento all'estero dell'italiano, Università degli studi de Trieste (Trieste: Lint, 1973), pp. 59–120.—Tr.

during the period. It seems to me that this new term reincorporated the notion of an active productivity that had been left behind when the Greek word *hermeneia* was translated by *interpretatio* and then later neglected by scholasticism—except perhaps in the "arts of preaching" from the end of the Middle Ages.

This humanist neologism, moreover, was the sign of profound ideological revisions. The old post-Roman and medieval notion of history as a tragic process of the "translation of empires" was replaced by a much more affirmative notion of temporality. Thus, the translator who brings to his vernacular language treasures from the past—whether it be a Bible or an encyclopedia—now offers his fellow citizens linguistic resources adequate to initiate positive action in a dynamic universe. The translator promulgates a political becoming, even a material prosperity, which is the natural goal of the *polis*. If meaning is supposed to enrich man's mind by circulating freely and abundantly in the language of present, lived experience, likewise gold and other material goods are supposed to circulate—thanks to commerce and *transportation*—just as blood has to circulate in the body (a frequent metaphor in the seventeenth century). Isn't the colonization of the New World basically a form of translation?

On the level of human psychology, this process of translation had to take subtler but no less important forms. Thanks to the *energeia* of speech (a word's capacity to make the image of a thing present to the mind), language can act on man's will and induce him to act. *Energeia* can also incite man to translate anger (*ira*) into a libidinal form (*concupiscentia*). This positive appetite transports man toward woman in *hymene*, allowing for a translation of semen, thanks to which the forms of life succeed each other. Thanatos becomes Eros. Through libidinal translation, nature manifests itself, over time, in its totality.

To refuse translation is to refuse life.

During the Renaissance, translators acquired their own god. He was called Proteus. Proteus was the son of Oceanus and

Neptune, and from the latter he received the gift of prophecy because he kept close watch over the monsters of the sea. Proteus is the very principle of mutability and transformation, two powers that are also the glory of man. Through translation, one lived experience is translated into another. Proteus contains Pan, the god of nature, which means that the totality of nature will not be expressed otherwise than in diversity.

Yet, this translation of nature into itself, however violent it may be, is not a redundancy or a simple repetition. It is a becoming, giving rise to the future; it is the principle of abundance and not of redundancy. In the city, this abundance is supposed to begin in the princes' discourses, thereby making possible many other kinds of abundance. Thus, the term *copia* ("abundance") replaced a more pejorative term—*amplificatio*—in the rhetorical theory of Erasmus, author of a rhetorical manual whose title begins with the words "De copia . . ." *Copia* is that figural capacity of discourse which allows man to express the diversity of his nature, as well as that of surrounding nature, and even to inaugurate mutations in its being. Without *copia,* there is only repetition. Erasmus says that repetition without diversity can be avoided if we acquire the capacity to translate a thought (*sententia*) into new forms more numerous than those assumed by Proteus himself.

Jacques Derrida said a moment ago that the philosophical operation is a process of translation. During the Renaissance, poets considered themselves also to be "translators," not only of a poetic legacy from past antiquity, but translators whose poetic performance was prophetic in the sense that it inaugurated a *future*. It seems to me that the philosopher Jacques Derrida aspires to something similar. If, however, during the Renaissance, rhetoric and poetry were considered to be the privileged instruments of human speculation, it was at the expense of philosophy. If Socrates is a good philosopher, it is because first of all he is eloquent; that is, the art of rhetoric makes Socrates' philosophical discourse effective. For a long time now in Derrida's writings, there has been a fascination with the poetic in the broadest sense. In "Plato's Pharmacy," poetic discourse is formally marked, and we cannot avoid being struck by its intrusion into philosophical discourse. If *Glas* can be considered a representative work, this trait is becoming more and more pronounced in Derrida's writings.

All of which leads me finally to my question: If poets, like philosophers, think they are the best translators, I would like to ask whether Jacques Derrida the poet is the master or the traitor of Jacques Derrida the philosopher!

What gives the philosophic message its specificity?

Jacques Derrida: *Reply*

Before getting to your final questions, I want to say that I subscribe entirely to the necessity you have signaled of rereading the history of the words "translation," "*hermeneia*," and so forth. Thus, I can only subscribe to what constitutes the totality of your presentation up to the end, thank you, and tell you I am in complete agreement. With respect to your final questions, there may nevertheless be some misunderstanding. As to what I was saying about the relation between philosophy and translation, I did not——

Eugene Vance

I meant to say, between philosophy and poetry as translating performances.

Jacques Derrida

Yes, but I did not say that philosophy was a translating performance. I said that the philosophic project was the project of a certain type of translation—translation interpreted in a certain manner. That's what I meant to say in "Plato's Pharmacy" and what I reiterated just a moment ago. That is, the philosophical act does not consist in a translating performance in that transformative or productive sense to which you have just referred. Rather, I was pointing to the idea of the fixation of a certain concept of translation: the idea that translation as the transportation of a meaning or of a truth from one language to another had to be possible, that univocality is possible, and so on—the whole classical *topos*, you see. When I said that philosophy was the thesis of translatability, I meant it not in the sense of translation as an active, poetic, productive, transformative "*hermeneia*," but rather in the sense of the transport of a univocal meaning, or in any case of a controllable plurivocality, into another linguistic element. In this regard, I was not at all passing myself off as a philosopher. It was, rather, an analysis. One could have done a critique of the philosophical claim to which I referred rather than praising anything whatsoever about the philosopher *qua* translator. This is where there has perhaps been a misunderstanding. Likewise, I wouldn't say that I am not at all a philosopher, but the utterances I proliferate around this problem are put forward from a position other than that of philosophy. This other position is not necessarily that of poetry either, but in any case it is not the position of philosophy. I ask questions of philosophy, and naturally this supposes a certain identification, a certain translation of myself into the body of a philosopher. But I don't feel that that's where I'm situated.

Eugene Vance

Allow me to rephrase my question. What is the place of a manifestly poetic performance in a text such as *Glas* or "Plato's Pharmacy"? Do you consider poetry to be subordinated finally to philosophical discourse, as Paul Ricoeur, for example, would claim?

Jacques Derrida: *Reply*

Yes, well, here I would say: Neither one nor the other. And I don't say that to evade your question easily. I think that a text like *Glas* is neither philosophic nor poetic. It circulates between these two genres, trying meanwhile to produce another text which would be of another genre or without genre. On the other hand, if one insists on defining genres at all costs, one could refer historically to Menippean satire, to "anatomy" (as in *The Anatomy of Melancholy*), or to something like philosophic parody where all genres—poetry, philosophy, theater, et cetera—are summoned up at once. Thus, if there is a genre, if it is absolutely necessary for there to be a genre within which to place the likes of *Glas*, then I think it is something like farce or Menippean satire, that is, a graft of several genres. I hope it's also something else that doesn't simply fall under either philosophy or what is called the poetic as both of these are classically understood. To do this, of course, I had to integrate into this corpus lots of limbs and pieces taken from the philosophical discourse. There is a whole book on Hegel; it's full of philosophy and literature, Mallarmé and Genet. Yet I myself do not read the genre of this body as either philosophic or poetic. This means that if your questions were addressed to the philosopher, I would have to say no. As for me, I talk about the philosopher, but I am not simply a philosopher. I say this even though, from an institutional point of view, I practice the trade of philosophy professor (under certain conditions which would have to be closely analyzed) and even though I believe that in a given historical, political situation of the university, it is necessary to fight so that something like philosophy remains possible. It is in this strategic context that on occasion I have spoken of philosophy's usefulness in translating or deciphering a certain number of things, such as what goes on in the media, and so on.

I will add just one more thing. It's a minor point in comparison with the essential part of your presentation to which, as I said, I totally subscribe and whose necessity I believe in. Your remark about "repudiating" deconstruction is a somewhat brutal translation of what I said yesterday. I said, without really insisting on it, that that word had been somewhat amplified beyond the point that I might perhaps have wished. In spite of that, I have not repudiated it. Moreover, I never repudiate anything, through either strength or weakness, I don't know which; but, whether it's my luck or my naiveté, I don't think I have ever repudiated anything. What I meant to say yesterday on the subject of deconstruction is that the fortune, let's say, of the word has surprised me. If I had been left all to myself, if I had been left alone with that word, I would not have given it as much importance. But finally, rightly or wrongly, I still believe in what was bound up with this word—I am not against it.

Claude Lévesque: *The Exile in Language*

It is difficult for me to let pass in silence and avoid under-scoring a fact that in itself may be insignificant: I am, today as yesterday, the only Quebecois who is participating in this roundtable discussion on translation. (Isn't Quebec a privi-leged place where an interminable case of translation is being tried and played out, a process of one-way meaning which, for that very reason, is a case of domination and appropriation? This, at least, is not insignificant.) I am also one of the only ones here (along with François Péraldi and perhaps Jacques Derrida as well—I don't know) whose maternal tongue is French. Yet, as we belong to such different milieux, is it really a question of the same language for each of us? Is there such a thing as the identity of a language? Does French usage some-where conform to the purity of an essence or an ideal? What can be said of the life and death of a language in language?

By underscoring this fact, this position of solitude—which, by the way, I put up with rather well—my solitude at this table but more broadly a solitude at the heart of the massively anglophone North American milieu, I am not trying to claim a privilege (solitude is neither a privilege nor a catastrophe). Nor am I trying to attract an easy, far too easy, sympathy or pity for our fate as Quebecois, for people who speak a lan-guage that has been humiliated, contaminated, dominated, and colonized, even though recently, perhaps forever, it has been peremptorily affirmed in its difference, its singularity, and its sovereignty. Rather, I simply want to ask a question that takes into account a position that is perhaps unique, perhaps universal, and perhaps also at once the one and the other.

Several Quebecois poets, as well as novelists and essayists, have tirelessly and tragically stated their distance from the maternal tongue, their nomadism and their discomfort in the language. Some have gone so far as to deny the very presence of a maternal tongue, as if the Quebecois writer (as well as the Quebecois people themselves) spoke—spoke to themselves—only from a position of exile in a foreign language that is irreducibly other and impossible to appropriate, as if they spoke only out of the approximation, incompleteness, injustice, and emptiness of a translation language. Thus, like anyone whose language has been expropriated, the Quebecois continues to cherish a nostalgia for a language that is his, a properly Quebecois language, a maternal tongue that will refashion an identity for him and reappropriate him to himself. It is a dream of fusion with the mother, with a tongue that is like a mother, that is, nearest at hand, nourishing, and reassuring. It is a dream to be at last joined in body with the mother language, to recognize himself in her who would recognize him, with the transparency, spontaneity, and truth of origins, without any risk, contamination, or domination.

This, then, is my question: What can one say of this curious relation to the maternal tongue where the latter never appears except as a translation language, one that is constantly being deported from a so-called original language that is itself, moreover, inaccessible and impossible to situate? Is this relation to language—let's call it "schizoid"—the normally abnormal relation to any language? Can language get us clear of any distance and any foreignness? I know that, for you, in order for any language to be a language, it can only be—structurally—a place of exile, a medium where absence, death, and repetition rule without exception. A language can only constitute itself as such by virtue of an original catastrophe, a violent separation from nature, a mortal and infinite fall putting us forever and since forever at a distance from the mother—any mother—destining us to the strangeness of that which has no homeland, no assignable limits, no origin, and no end.

If this is the way it is, one can speak the maternal tongue only as another's language. As you have written in "Living On": "A tongue can never be appropriated; it is only ever as the other's tongue that it is mine, and reciprocally." The maternal tongue could therefore only be the language of the bad mother (but there would be no good one), that is, of the mother who has always already weaned her child, who keeps her distance, far off (*fort*), and whom one would vainly and repeatedly try to make come back (*da*). The figure of the mother could only be disfigured, fragmented, and dismantled in language, figuring only that which is not or that which is baseless and faceless. Language would be always already abandoned to its own devices, bastardized, betrayed, contaminated, and foreign. The purity of language (of any language and thus also of the so-called Quebecois language) receives here a mortal blow. The crisis arises, Mallarmé said, from the fact that "*on a touché au vers.*"* Here, let us say, language has been tampered with, and as a result its whole system has been shaken, in particular the illusion, as far as language is concerned, of appropriation, specularization, mastery, and identification.

For the Quebecois writer, this estrangement in relation to language, this lack of mother tongue in a tongue that nevertheless lacks for nothing, is a torment, to be sure, and an untenable contradiction. It can lead to silence, paralysis, and even madness. Yet, it must be said, this expropriation and expatriation are also perhaps a chance: the possibility (and impossibility) of reinventing language as if from the beginning. We should not forget that the current of everyday language hurries by and goes beyond. To be sure, it hollows out its riverbed, but it also overflows it constantly. No shore, no limit can hold back its breaking waves. It is a question, then, of widening language, of casting it off and sending it back out to the wide open sea, of

---

*"Poetry has been tampered with," but also it has been "touched upon," "reached," "attained."—Tr.

releasing its safety catches so it can venture forth beyond its limits into absolute danger, in the direction of the fascinating unknown which is forever out of reach. Doesn't the writer begin writing at the moment words escape him, when familiar words become once again unknown? Doesn't he write in order to translate silence—without breaking it—into writing, in order to bring to ordinary language the dignity of a translated language (that language we lack which always appears more melodious, more sonorous, more concrete, richer in its images than our own, and therefore sacred, so to speak)? Whoever reinvents the tongue, the maternal tongue, doesn't he break with both the materialism of language and the paternal law that kept him at a distance from it? This is a question I am asking you—of you, with you, and almost in your own terms. What is to be said of the situation of the (Quebecois) writer in his/her language?

Jacques Derrida: *Reply*

I agree that it is time for us to take our bearings from the linguistic place in which we find ourselves, this strange linguistic place that is Quebec where, after all, the problem of translation is posed in forms and with a force, a character, and an urgency—in particular a political urgency—that are altogether singular. I think that if anything in this colloquium constitutes an event, it is in relation to the linguistic position of Quebec, where, at every moment, at every step, texts arrive not only in translation—that's obviously the case everywhere—but in a translation that is remarked and underscored. One has only to walk down the street or go to a café and right away one receives utterances in several different languages (such as French or English on publicity posters, et cetera). Or else several languages—sometimes there are three— intersect each other within the same utterance. For the last two or three days, I have experienced utterances in three languages in a single sentence, and it is this, after all, that makes for the singularity of what is going on for us right now, as well as the fact that the participants at this roundtable are themselves in a very particular linguistic situation. By going around the table, we could remark the fact that not one of us is like a fish in water in the language he or she is speaking. Unless I am mistaken, not one of the subjects at this table speaks French as his or her maternal tongue, except perhaps two of us. And, even then, you [Péraldi] are French; I'm not. I come from Algeria. I have therefore still another relation to the French tongue. But still, it would be amusing to analyze the complexity, the internal translation to which our bodies are continuously submitting, here, at this moment.

Donald Bouchard: *Question from the Floor*

I want to come back to the idea of the double bind which you have introduced. It seems to me that in the end what the double bind indicates is a closed system from which one cannot escape. Madness is a Babelian idea which does not teach us anything about God's power, the history of the *logos*, and thus the idea of power. Yet power encloses individuals. One way of asking my first question would thus be: Is it possible to find a way out of madness? One can understand madness on the basis of the "capacity" to get out of it—and is there a way out of it? I would also like to ask another question about Walter Benjamin. It concerns the way in which one generally thinks of translation, that is, the idea that an original is always presumed and that the "something" coming after is never as good as what comes first. It is in this manner that you have introduced words such as "sacred" and "nostalgia."

Jacques Derrida

I'm not the one who introduced them.

Donald Bouchard

My second question is this: Is it necessary to have sacred texts and is a perfect translation possible? I think that translation is always a manner of introducing an imperfection. Can one regard translation as the introduction of an imperfection from one culture to another?

Jacques Derrida

To respond, or rather not to respond but to resonate with your first question: I don't know if one can get out. I don't think there is any sense in always wanting to get out. One can get out for a moment, but actually I don't know whether madness consists in not being able to get out or in wanting to get out. Basically, what form does an exit take? All one can say is that in every closed place, there are things called "exits," and that's what defines it as a closed place. To this first type of question—and I am not sure I have understood very well where it was going—I cannot reply.

Concerning your allusions to Benjamin and the question about the necessity of sacred texts, I am going to be very prudent—and not only by refusing to take responsibility for Benjamin's text. It's true that there are things in that text which can make one uncomfortable and which begin with the sacred text, insist on the messianic character of translation, and so on. Yet, a sacred text, if there is such a thing, is a text that does not await the question of whether or not it is necessary that there be such a thing: if there is a sacred text, then there is a sacred text. You are wondering whether or not the sacred text is necessary: this is a question which that text couldn't care less about. The sacred text happens, it is an event, if there is such a thing, and it doesn't wait for anyone to accept the idea that there may be such a thing. It's an event, and that's what Benjamin means. One always has to postulate an original. This may look like a very classical position and basically like a distinction between the original and the translated version. This appearance is very reassuring, but at the same time, in a less classical and less reassuring manner, Benjamin often says that one recognizes the difference between a translation and an original in that the original can be translated several times but a translation cannot be retranslated. Despite the fact that we know of examples of translations that have been re-translated, when this occurs—when, for example, one trans-lates [Friedrich] Hölderlin's translation of Sophocles—the first translation, if it has the force of an event, becomes an original. There is always a structure of "original translation" even when translations are retranslated. This does not mean that Benjamin kneels before the existence of sacred texts, that he bases what he says on the dogma of the existence of the sacred text. Perhaps what he is saying to us is this: Every time the event of an untranslatable text occurs, every time there is a text that is not totally translatable, in other words, every time there is a proper name, it gets sacralized. It is this process of sacralization that has to be explained. Benjamin tells us that sacralization or the sacred is the untranslatable, and every time there is some proper name in the language that does not let itself become totally common, that cannot be translated, one is dealing with a text that is beginning to be sacralized. One is dealing with poetry. This is why Benjamin refers litera-ture or poetry to a religious or sacred model, because he thinks that if there is something untranslatable in literature (and, in a certain way, literature is the untranslatable), then it is sacred. If there is any literature, it is sacred; it entails sacral-ization. This is surely the relation we have to literature, in spite of all our denegations in this regard. The process of sacralization is underway whenever one says to oneself in dealing with a text: Basically, I can't transpose this text such as it is into another language; there is an idiom here; it is a work; all the efforts at translation that I might make, that it itself calls forth and demands, will remain, in a certain way and at a given moment, vain or limited. This text, then, is a sacred text. Thus, perhaps Benjamin does not begin with reli-gion, that is, with the posited existence of such-and-such a sacred text by the history of religions. Perhaps he wants to explain what a sacred text is, how one sacralizes a text, and how any text, to the extent that it brings with it a proper-name effect, is on its way to becoming sacred. At this point, then,

one doesn't have to wonder whether sacred texts are necessary. There is sacredness; and if there is sacredness, then it
looks like this. In this sense, that text one is reading is both
unique and a paradigmatic example which gives the law and
in which one reads the law of sacralization—that's how it
always is. There is Babel everywhere. Every time someone
says his or her own name or creates a literary work or imposes
a signature, even though it is translatable and untranslatable,
he or she produces something sacred, not just some prose like
Monsieur Jourdain* who makes prose. On the contrary, when
one does something poetic, one makes for sacredness and in
that sense one produces the untranslatable.

Now, to be sure, the problem becomes more serious and
more acute in the type of answer I am giving you, that is,
when I say that there are processes of sacralization and to
account for them one must begin with these problems of translation, of language, and of the limits on translation. My discourse here is one that is not very respectful of the sacred
because it says: We're going to explain how sacralization,
which is everywhere, happens; here is how it comes about, et
cetera. On the other hand, someone who receives the sacred as
an event and before trying to explain it says: Okay, I believe
on faith that this particular text—either the Gospels or the Old
Testament—is not an example in which to study the processes of sacralization; these texts are absolute events which
took place only once and I am answerable to them. This is
someone who would say: No, one does not begin with the
processes of sacralization in order to study the sacred; one
begins with the sacred, which has already taken place and
whose event is explained only with reference to itself, in order
then to better understand history. I don't know if what I am
saying is clear. My point is that there are two apparently incompatible attitudes with regard to the sacred. One tries to
understand the genesis of the sacred and sacralization. It be-

---

*Molière's bourgeois gentleman who, upon learning that everything which
is not poetry is prose, exclaims: "So, I am speaking prose!"—Tr.

gins with sacralization in order to understand the sacred. The other says: No, the sacred is not sacralization; it begins by happening; first there were the prophets, Babel, or the Gospels, and then there is sacralization. Thus, everything I've recounted here can take on another meaning if one believes sacralization has its meaning in the sacred rather than the other way around. The debate here is open-ended: the only response is the event. Also, don't forget that for Benjamin the limit on translation (the sacred text in which the sense and the letter can no longer be dissociated) is both the untranslatable and the *pure* translatable, the place and the appeal for translation, the model (*Urbild*) of all translation—the "intralinear translated version" of the sacred text. It translates without translating; it translates itself in the original. I don't know if I have answered your question.

Monique Bosco: *Question from the Floor*

I have been struck by something. Since you have spoken a good deal about psychoanalysis, I would like to talk a little about repression. I received a sheet distributed by the Department of French Studies that asked anyone who wanted to participate in these roundtable discussions to read certain texts which were to serve as the basis for the two sessions. One was a very beautiful text by Derrida ["Living On: Borderlines"] which he has not yet published——

Jacques Derrida

Yes, it has been published in translation. It's a text that was written in French but which I knew would appear first in English, so it is marked by this particular address. It appeared a few days ago in the United States.

Monique Bosco

The others are very important, very difficult texts by Blanchot: *Death Sentence* and "The Madness of the Day." This was an opportunity to have a translation or an interpretation of these two Blanchot texts by Derrida. I notice, however (is it by chance or as a result of repression?), that no one has mentioned them. These texts interest me very much, particularly the passage on the rose or the gypsum flower inscribed in the text, which, in my opinion, is something fundamental. I wanted to ask about the problem of translating poetry, a problem that Henri Meschonnic already raised several years ago when he talked about "traducia Celan." Once again, it is a question of someone who has to die for his work to be made available to us. This, in a nutshell, is the problem of the translation of a poet. The [French] translation of _Niemandsrose_ [_The No-One's-Rose_] came out for the first time this year. The work of Paul Celan, who was also exiled in his language, is an extremely disturbing problem, I think, one that could concern all of us. How does one translate these sacred texts—since a poetic text is almost always sacred—especially the text of someone exiled from his own language, just as [Franz] Kafka was? Given that we are, after all, in those disciplines that are concerned with the sacred text which is poetry, I was wondering how it is that it has been pushed aside, avoided, repressed? Isn't it the case that, even when one translates, integrally or by extracts, one adopts a particular way of translating, but in an absolute fashion? Doesn't the problem of translation pass by way of the translator's sex? In this case, the French translation of _Niemandsrose_ was done by a woman. In another case, that of the American poet Sylvia Plath, both women and a man have translated her work. . . . In _Death Sentence_, the woman lover is a translator (as in the case of Kafka and Milena).* Must the woman always be not only the poet's servant but the poet's translator as well? It's a problem that's been around for a long time, since I noticed while reading about Stendhal that he also said to women: Don't write, translate, and you will earn an honorable living. Thus it's a whole political question.

---

*Milena Jesenská-Polak, who translated some of Kafka's works into Czech.—Tr.

Jacques Derrida

If one refers to a certain concept of translation that prevailed up until Benjamin perhaps, the concept according to which translation is derivative, or in a position of derivation in relation to an original that is itself seminal, then the fact that women are often translators or that they are invited to do so (objectively, statistics would show that they are often in the position of translators), this fact, in effect, comes out of a subordination which poses a political problem. I don't want to insist on this—it's obvious to everyone. If, however, one displaces somewhat the concept of translation on the basis, for example, of what Eugene Vance did just a moment ago, or from a perspective that would see translation as something other than a secondary operation, at that moment the position of the woman translator would be something else, even though it would still be marked sexually. One must not fail to notice that Benjamin uses the term "translator" in the masculine and not in the feminine. I believe this is consonant with the whole system of his text. He speaks of the translator, not of the woman translator, and the translator in general can be either a man or a woman. It is in this general sense that Benjamin presents the translator. If one displaces this classical perspective, one becomes conscious—from within that classical perspective and from within the text I'm talking about—that the so-called original is in a position of demand with regard to the translation. The original is not a plenitude which would come to be translated by accident. The original is in the situation of demand, that is, of a lack or exile. the original is indebted a priori to the translation. Its survival is a demand and a desire for translation, somewhat like the Babelian demand: Translate me. Babel is a man, or rather a male god, a god that is not full since he is full of resentment, jealousy, and so on. He calls out, he desires, he lacks, he calls for the complement or the supplement or, as Benjamin says, for that which will come along to enrich him. Translation does not come along in addition, like an accident added to a full substance; rather, it is what the original text demands—and not simply the signatory of the original text but the text itself. If the translation is indebted to the original (this is its task, its debt [*Aufgabe*]), it is because already the original is indebted to the coming translation. This means that translation is also the law. There is a dissymmetry here but it's a double dissymmetry, with the result that the woman translator in this case is not simply subordinated, she is not the author's secretary. She is also the one who is loved by the author and on whose basis alone writing is possible. Translation is writing; that is, it is not translation only in the sense of transcription. It is a productive writing called forth by the original text. Thus, as in Blanchot's texts (*Death Sentence* as well as "The Madness of the Day"), woman is on the side of the affirming law rather than only in that derivative situation you have spoken of. And, in effect, this is what is going on and what one can read in *Death Sentence*: the woman translator can be translated as secondary, subordinated, oppressed femininity, but one can also translate her as absolutely desirable, the one who makes the law, truth, and so forth. This possibility can be read in *Death Sentence*, in "The Madness of the Day"—it can be read even in Benjamin if one makes a special effort. All of this means that the political problem, which seems to me inevitable and real, has a very complex strategy. All of its terms must be laid out again; one must rethink translation——

Monique Bosco

Yes, that's clear. On the other hand, however, do you agree that there is a problem of sexual difference which enters in at the level of translation? Only one of my books has been translated by a man, and it was a completely different book.

Jacques Derrida

And that's because a man translated it?

Monique Bosco

I'm beginning to think so. [Laughter.]

Jacques Derrida

It's altogether possible. I'm convinced you're right to ask the question, but the analysis of the effects remains very tricky. When you raised the question of sexuality in translation, I was thinking of something else. I was thinking of what happens when one has to translate sexed personal pronouns with un-sexed ones. Let me explain what I mean. At the end of *Death Sentence,* there is a passage where Blanchot says first of all "*la pensée,*" and it is clear that he is talking about "thought." Then there is a slippage which takes one to the last line of the text where he writes: "*Et à elle, je dis 'viens' et éternellement elle est là* ["And to that thought I say eternally, 'Come,' and eternally it is there"]. From the grammatical point of view (and one can follow the grammatical and rhetorical order of the text leading to the grammatical point of view), the feminine pronoun "*elle*" unquestionably refers to "*la pensée*" or "thought." Yet, obviously Blanchot has played on the "*elle,*" or he has let it play, let it slip toward "*elle*" or "she." In English, naturally, a rigorous translation must relate "*elle*" to "*pensée*" so that it becomes "it." At that moment, the text totally caves in. More-over, in the existing translation of *Death Sentence,* this is just what happened: the "*elle*" at the end—which is a sublime "*elle*"—is crushed, broken down by the necessity for a gram-matically rigorous translation. There are problems like this all the time in translating from French to English as well as be-tween German and French. When the translator becomes aware of the problem, he can of course add a note* or else put words in brackets, but what he is doing at that point is not an operation of translation: commentaries, analyses, warnings are not translations. Thus, one also has to consider the *economic* problem of translation. Basically, to produce an ideal translation, which would be only a translation and nothing else, one would have to translate one word by one word. As soon as one puts two or three words in the place of one, translation becomes an analytic explicitation; that is, it is no longer strictly speaking a translation. To translate "*elle*" by "it," then, without losing too much, one must add a note, thereby giving in to a work of interpretation which spoils the economy of translation strictly speaking—linguistic translation. This is the quantitative problem of translation, which we haven't talked about very much or even at all. Yet it is, I think, a central problem.

André Beaudet: *Question from the Floor*

I have several questions. The one I will ask first is banal and simple: Do we or do you always translate by ear? In what way is a translation an autotranslation which consists in turning something uncanny or unfamiliar around in order to make oneself understood as in a familiar context but still otherwise? I would assimilate this autotranslation to something I've heard for the last three days—certain effects of a third ear, for example, a third mouth, a third tongue, or a third position be-

---

*But can any note take up the slack here, in this situation? In his essay on Benjamin's "The Task of the Translator," Blanchot writes: "The translator is indeed a strange, nostalgic man: he experiences in his own language, but in the manner of something missing, everything promised him in the way of present affirmations by the original work (the work which remains more-over—he can't quite reach it since he's not at home, at rest in its language but is an eternal guest who doesn't live there). That's why, if we can believe the testimony of specialists, he is always in more difficulty as he translates with the language to which he belongs than at a loss with the one he doesn't possess" ("Traduire," in *L'Amitié*, p. 72; my translation).—Tr.

_____

tween philosophy and poetry. It is a question here not of simple listening but of an attention that has a cutting edge to the extent that, as Nietzsche says in *Beyond Good and Evil*, with this third ear one "handles his language like a supple blade and feels from his arm down to his toes the perilous delight of the quivering, over-sharp steel that wants to bite, hiss, cut." These three words—bite, hiss, cut—already comprehend some of the operations that you have translated into your work.

Jacques Derrida

I am having trouble translating your last question to myself. I've received it, but I have not understood it very well, if by understanding one means being able to reproduce and translate it. Like everyone, I always try, I think, to translate or to translate myself—to autotranslate—which includes that gesture of appropriation that is part of translation. However, if you have seen or noticed or heard a third ear for the last few days, then it may be that this operation of autotranslation is impossible. I am conscious of it in part. It is less a question of autotranslation turned back in on itself, trying to master the *Unheimliche* or the uncanny so that it becomes simply the familiar, than it is of the opposite movement. But this is not to say that one has to turn oneself over, bound hand and foot, to the *Unheimliche*, because I don't believe in that. In other words, I don't believe in seeking out absolute risk, absolute nonreappropriation, alienation, and madness for their own sake, and, besides, I don't want to have anything to do with that. I'm too afraid of it. What I was trying to do was work out a kind of economy with the means at hand, an economy that would not be one of a maniacal and "self-centered"* autotranslation. Let's say I was trying also to produce texts that produce other ears, in a certain way—ears that I don't see or hear myself, things that don't come down to me or come back to me. A text, I believe, does not come back. I have insisted a

_____
*In English in the original.—Tr.

lot on this theme, and I am doing it once more: I have tried to write texts that don't return and don't allow for retranslation. I can't retranslate any more than anyone else can, so I'm not extolling what I do. I don't believe one can retranslate one's own utterances in an exhaustive fashion. It's better to produce texts that leave and don't come back altogether, but that are not simply and totally alienated or foreign. One regulates an economy with one's texts, with other subjects, with one's family, children, desire. They take off on their own, and one then tries to get them to come back a little even as they remain outside, even as they remain the other's speech. This is what happens when one writes a text. _Mutatis mutandis_, it's like a child—an old _topos_ which has its historical patent of nobility. But a child is not only that toward which or for which a father or mother remains; it is an other who starts talking and goes on talking by itself, without your help, who doesn't even answer you except in your fantasy. You think it's talking to you, that you are talking in it, but in fact it talks by itself. On this basis, one constructs paternity or maternity fantasies; one says that, after all, it's still one's own, that life is sweet, et cetera. Finally, however, if one is still a little attentive to the _anankē_ that we were talking about earlier, one knows that children don't belong to us but we console ourselves with the fantasy that they do. Like everyone, then, I have fantasies of children and of texts. That's how I work things out with the uncanny. I don't know if I have met your question.

André Beaudet

If your own text comes back as a kind of echo, I was wondering whether it was possible for someone else to plug into your work. Is it possible to write on the basis of your work?

Jacques Derrida

What does that mean: "on the basis of"? On the basis of means starting from, which is to say going away from. As to what you called an echo: There are, in effect, echoes. It would be interesting to analyze closely what happens when a text you write comes back to you in one form or another. What does it mean: "to come back"? It means that another makes use of it or cites it. I've had this happen to me. Taking the situation here for the last two days as one to analyze, I've functioned a little like the "original." (It's true—one mustn't try to hide such things from oneself.) Each of you has taken the floor, then I have spoken after each of you has, and, after all, I'm the one who has been quoted most often, so that these things have come back to me. But it would be necessary to analyze very closely the experience of hearing someone else read a text you have allegedly written or signed. All of a sudden someone puts a text right in front of you again, in another context, with an intention that is both somewhat yours and not simply yours. Each time it happens, it's a very curious, very troubling experience. I can't analyze it here. What I can say is that it is never the same text, never an echo, that comes back to you. It can be a very pleasant or a very unpleasant experience. It can reconcile you with what you've done, make you love it or hate it. There are a thousand possibilities. Yet one thing is certain in all this diversity, and that is that it's never the same. What is more, even before someone cites or reads it to you, as in the present situation, the text's identity has been lost, and it's no longer the same as soon as it takes off, as soon as it has begun, as soon as it's on the page. By the end of the sentence, it's no longer the same sentence that it was at the beginning. Thus, in this sense, there is no echo, or, if there is, it's always distorted. Perhaps the desire to write is the desire to launch things that come back to you as much as possible in as many forms as possible. That is, it is the desire to perfect a program or a matrix having the greatest potential, variability, undecidability, plurivocality, et cetera, so that each time something returns it will be as different as possible. This is also what one does when one has children—talking beings who can always outtalk you. You have the illusion that it comes back to you, that it comes from you—that these unpredictable words come out of you somewhat. This is what goes on with texts. When I saw, for example, that it was a piece of "Living On" that Donato was quoting, I was reading it through Donato's text: it was something very strange which returned utterly without me. I thought: That's not bad, but it's not the same. It's never the same *in any case*, and it never returns. This is both a bad thing and a good thing. Obviously, if it came back, that would also be terrible. One wants it to return exactly like it is, but then one also knows very well that if it did come back exactly like it is, one would have only one wish and that is to run away.

Nicole Bureau: *Question from the Floor*

Doesn't the work of Blanchot seem, in some way, to be a "fictional" practice of translation? The titles never seem definitive. The "mood," the space, and the rhythm of his speech are continually transformed, as if in order to prevent writing from fixing its object (or settling on its objective). There is no "first" text, but there is also no definitive—or unique—version which would have the force of law by guaranteeing the writing's seal. The only thing "proper" to Blanchot's writing is the unflagging search for his language, his "genre" (theory? fiction?), or his name.

Would it be possible to see a relation between "recitation"— to which you have already alluded, most notably in *Pas*—and translation? Both of them are linked to the work of repetition, and both of them are also undone by repetition.

Doesn't this generalized practice of dividing language in two manifest itself in a singular fashion in *Death Sentence*? Certain names, which are first fragmented or reduced to their initials, suddenly come back up to the surface of the *récit* where they already disturb the reading of the narrative text; others have no specific identity and are dressed now in the feminine, now in the masculine (I am thinking of Simon/Simone, among others).

What do you think of these various manifestations of Blanchot's work?

Jacques Derrida

I completely agree. Indeed, all he has done is to translate translation in the most enigmatic sense. He does this not only through multiple versions but sometimes by very small modifications. Sometimes it is the mention of the word "*récit*" or "novel" that simply disappears; or else he deletes one little page from the end, leaving the rest of the text intact; or still other times there are massive mutations, as with *Thomas the Obscure*, where, of the 350 pages crammed into the first version, he retains something very economical, 120 or 150 pages, for the second version. What is remarkable is that, in spite of everything, this translation and this transformation, even when they erase something, keep the memory or the trace of what they are erasing. The version is not a translation that comes from the original and—how to put it?—from which comes the original as if there was *here* an original and *there* a translation. No; there is an increase. The second translation of *Death Sentence* keeps the trace of the erasure in the erasure itself. The memory of all the versions is archived, as in the Library of Congress. It is a still larger language, as Benjamin would say: it is an increased corpus which has grown from the original to the translation, from the first to the second version.

As for proper names in Blanchot, they are at once apparently insignificant names which are then loaded with a thousand possible translations and meanings. I mentioned Thomas. Well, there is an immense implicit discourse on Thomas' proper name. One has to interpret the *récit* as the translation of the proper name into the story which transforms it into a common name. One finds there a translation of Thomas' proper name beginning with the biblical references, the character of the double Thomas, of Didyme, of Thomas the Obscure. Since Thomas' surname—the Obscure—is a common noun qualifier, one can see the whole *récit* as a translation, in a certain way, of the proper name. One could also talk about the initials in *Death*

Sentence. The *J* can be translated right away into Jesus and then into a number of other things. Natalie can also be translated into Jesus, since it signifies Noel, Nativity. Thus, in a certain sense the proper name is pregnant with the *récit*, which can be interpreted as a translation of the proper name.

Claude Lévesque

We must necessarily bring to a close this exchange which, all the same, is infinite and thank Jacques Derrida very warmly. His passage among us will have been an *event*, but the kind of event that is much more ahead of us than already behind us. I speak as the interpreter—the translator—for each one of us when I say to him: Thanks for many things—for coming, for his generosity which each one of us has so clearly felt, for the total and careful attention he has brought to each of us. Finally, we thank him for being what he is. A question still remains in the end: Who is he? Who is Jacques Derrida? Perhaps we may venture to answer by saying that he is unique and innumerable, like all of us, differently than all of us.

Jacques Derrida

I too want to thank you for your presence, your attention, your patience. This is not just a polite formula on my part, but a real sign of gratitude. Thank you.

Works Cited

Abraham, Nicolas. "The Shell and the Kernel." Translated by Nicolas Rand. *Diacritics*, Spring 1979.

Abraham, Nicolas, and Maria Torok. *Cryptonymie: Le Verbier de l'Homme aux loups*. Paris: Aubier-Flammarion, 1976.

_____. *L'Ecorce et le noyau*. Paris: Aubier-Flammarion, 1978.

Benjamin, Walter. "The Task of the Translator." In *Illuminations*. Translated by Harry Zohn. New York: Schocken Books, 1969.

Blanchot, Maurice. *L'Amitié*. Paris: Gallimard, 1971.

_____. *Death Sentence*. Translated by Lydia Davis. Barrytown, N.Y.: Station Hill Press, 1978.

_____. "The Madness of the Day." Translated by Lydia Davis. *Triquarterly* 40 (Fall 1977).

_____. *Le Pas au-delà*. Paris: Gallimard, 1973.

Derrida, Jacques. *La Carte postale*. Paris: Aubier-Flammarion, 1980. (Includes the essays "Du tout," and "Legs de Freud.")

_____. "Fors." Translated by Barbara Johnson. *The Georgia Review*, Spring 1977.

_____. "Freud and the Scene of Writing." In *Writing and Difference*. Translated by Alan Bass. Chicago: University of Chicago Press, 1978.

_____. *Glas*. Paris: Galilée, 1974.

_____. "Ja, ou le faux-bond." *Digraphe* 11 (April 1977).

_____. "Living On: Borderlines." Translated by James Hulbert. In *Deconstruction and Criticism*. New York: Seabury Press, 1979.

_____. *Margins of Philosophy*. Translated by Alan Bass. Chicago: University of Chicago Press, 1982.

163

_____. "Me—Psychoanalysis: An Introduction to 'The Shell and the Kernel' by Nicolas Abraham." Translated by Richard Klein. *Diacritics*, Spring 1979.

_____. *Of Grammatology*. Translated by Gayatri Chakravorty Spivak. Baltimore: Johns Hopkins University Press, 1974.

_____. "La Parole soufflée." In *Writing and Difference*. Translated by Alan Bass. Chicago: University of Chicago Press, 1978.

_____. *Pas. Gramma* 3/4 (1976).

_____. "Plato's Pharmacy." In *Dissemination*. Translated by Barbara Johnson. Chicago: University of Chicago Press, 1981.

_____. *Positions*. Translated by Alan Bass. Chicago: University of Chicago Press, 1978.

_____. *Signéponge/Signsponge*. Translated by Richard Rand. New York: Columbia University Press, 1984.

_____. *Speech and Phenomena*. Translated by David B. Allison. Evanston, Ill.: Northwestern University Press, 1973.

_____. *Spurs: Nietzsche's Styles*. Translated by Barbara Harlow. Chicago: University of Chicago Press, 1979.

Freud, Sigmund. *The Complete Psychological Works: Standard Edition*. 24 vols. Edited and translated by James Strachey. New York: W. W. Norton, 1976.

Kofman, Sarah. "Un Philosophe 'Unheimlich.' " In *Ecarts: Quatre Essais à propos de Jacques Derrida*. Paris: Fayard, 1973.

Neitzsche, Friedrich. *Ecce Homo*. Translated by Walter Kaufmann. New York: Vintage Books, 1969.

_____. *The Portable Nietzsche*. Translated by Walter Kaufmann. New York: Viking Press, 1954.

_____. *On the Future of Our Educational Institutions*. Translated by J. M. Kennedy. In *The Complete Works of Friedrich Nietzsche*, vol. 3. Edited by Oscar Levy. New York: Russell & Russell, 1964.

Winnicott, Donald. *Playing and Reality*. New York: Basic Books, 1971.